"This bright and gracious work is so clear in its intent and organization that it instantly seems a film instruction classic and a must for any visual artist as well as filmmaker. Ms. Begleiter defines image making with so much clarity as to open a new door in one's mind. The book speaks: This is what you do and how, now get going!"

Richard Hoover
Production Designer: *Girl, Interrupted; Dead Man Walking*

"A wonderfully logical book about a precise tool to use in an illogical medium. Marcie Begleiter's process is a visual and organizational assist to any filmmaker trying to shift from story in words to story in moving image."

Joan Tewkesbury
Screenwriter: *Nashville, Thieves Like Us*
Director: *Felicity*

"*From Word to Image* is wonderful. It examines the how-to's of storyboard art and is full of rich film history. It demystifies an aspect of filmmaking that benefits everyone involved: from directors, to cinematographers, to production designers."

Joe Petricca
Vice Dean, AFI Conservatory

"Finally! A definitive book for directors and producers to learn and appreciate the great support of story-boarding. In TV, where getting enough prep time is a rarity, working with a storyboard artist saves your life and your budget. *From Word to Image* reveals the process of visualization and focused storytelling. I am thrilled to add it to my library."

Nancy Malone
Co-founder, Women in Film

"*From Word to Image* delivers a clear explanation of the tools available to help a director tell his story visually, effectively, and efficiently—it could be subtitled 'A Director Prepares.' "

Bruce Bilson
Emmy Award-winning director of over 350 television episodes

"Marcie Begleiter has put together an energized learning tool and superb visual guide to better visual communication. Sharing learned skills and clear process organization, Marcie gives us insight into how to create a focused developmental blueprint for production. *From Word to Image* will inspire you to clear your concept and vision, then go on to refine and communicate ideas."

Jan Hastings
Creative Director
Lightspan Interactive

"*From Word To Image* can create a major difference in visual awareness for writers, producers, and directors. It indicates a language which guides filmmakers to find appropriate pictures for the narrative story. It nurtures the communication of the crew to fuse the story and image into a symphony. As a producer I think that the book would be a gift for writers attempting to visualize their scenes. And it's great fun to read!"

Rita Nasser, Executive Producer
ZDF, German Public Television

"The critically important and intricate process of visual design in filmmaking has been hidden from aspiring artists too long. Marcie Begleiter's book offers a refreshing level of clarity and practical instruction about the most mysterious aspect of creative collaboration on film. Her experience and exemplary reputation as a mentor for film students makes this book a wonderful journey of discovery."

Robert W. Peterson
Chairman, Department of Film, Art Center College of Design

MICHAEL WIESE PRODUCTIONS
www.mwp.com

Since 1981, Michael Wiese Productions has been dedicated to providing novice and seasoned filmmakers with vital information on all aspects of filmmaking and videomaking. We have published more than 50 books, used in over 500 film schools worldwide.

Our authors are successful industry professionals — they believe that the more knowledge and experience they share with others, the more high-quality films will be made. That's why they spend countless hours writing about the hard stuff: budgeting, financing, directing, marketing, and distribution. Many of our authors, including myself, are often invited to conduct filmmaking seminars around the world.

We truly hope that our publications, seminars, and consulting services will empower you to create enduring films that will last for generations to come.

We're here to help. Let us hear from you.

Sincerely,

Michael Wiese
Publisher, Filmmaker

Image

FromW

Storyboarding and the Filmmaking Process

by
Marcie Begleiter

ord to Image

Published by Michael Wiese
Productions
11288 Ventura Blvd.
Suite 821
Studio City, CA 91604

818. 379.8799
Fax: 818. 986.3408
mw@mwp.com
www.mwp.com

Printed and Manufactured
in the United Startes of America

Library of Congress
Cataloging-in-Publication Data

Begleiter, Marcie.
From Word To Image: storyboarding
and the filmmaking process/
Marcie Begleiter.
p.cm.
Includes bibliographical references
and index.
ISBN 0-941188-28-0
1. Storyboards. 2. Commercial
art Technique. I. Title.

NC1002S85 B44 200
741.6--dc21

Cover Design: Art Hotel, Los Angeles
Back Cover Photo: Susan Sheriden
Interior Layout: William Morosi
Printed by: McNaughton & Gunn

Table of Contents

For
Jeff and Zachary

"First, I storyboarded it."

acknowledgements

There have been many people who have helped in the research, writing, and editing of this book. I would like to thank the librarians at the film archives of UCLA, USC, AFI, The Lilly Research Library of the Academy of Motion Pictures Arts and Sciences, and the Museum of Modern Art for their help in tracking down many of the storyboard examples in this volume. In addition, Helen Cohen and the DeMille estate were very gracious in allowing me to photograph their collection. Many of the quotes and interviews in the book have been newly transcribed from interviews conducted over the past two years. I want to extend thanks to Harold and Lillian Michelson, Robert Boyle, Robert Wise, Gene Allen, John Jensen, Richard Hoover, Joe Musso, John Mann, Frank Gladstone, Ron Gress, and John Coven for their time and cooperation.

I would also like to thank the estate of Alfred Hitchcock and Leland H. Faust for his help in securing the rights to reproduce material from the collection which is held by the Lilly Library. George Roy Hill has generously allowed us to reproduce his drawings and Edwin Brown was most helpful in helping to secure that release. The chapter on job opportunites was enhanced by the comments of Cynthia Paskos and Gina Mandela of Local 790 and the agents Mark Milller and Philip Mittel.

A project this size is rarely accomplished solo and I'd like to express thanks to Gary Perkovac and Peter Carpenter for their aid with the illustrations, Channee Edwards for helping to round up the clearances and Vee Vitanza, David Neeham, and Grant Powell for their work on the appendix of Web sites.

The crew at Michel Wiese Productions has been a support all along the way. I especially want to thank Michael for suggesting this project and not taking no for an answer. Lisa Wexton has given me editorial as well as moral support throughout; Milena Albert and Ken Lee have helped to keep the project well-organized and on deadline. B. J. Markel helped to add the final polish.

A word also to Chris Craig and his team at the AFI Professional Training Division for the long-term support of my work and their willingness to make creative leaps in the service of film education. Also, Bob Petersen, the chairman of the film department at Art Center College of Art and Design, has helped to support and develop the classes from which this book grows. The Faculty Council at Art Center supported the book with a generous grant that helped to pay for the image clearances. And last but certainly not least I want to thank Anita Hyshiver for her many months of advice and insights into this mysterious process of bringing forth a book where nothing stood before.

prologue

In the winter of 1984 I found myself on a film set on Cape Cod. A scenic design company had sent me to paint sets for a film that was about to shoot in Provencetown, Mass. I was a struggling artist, showing sporadically in the art galleries of Boston and taking on theater design and craft gigs to pay my studio rent.

One day while hanging out on top of a ladder I overheard a conversation between the director and the production office back in Los Angeles. He was vigorously requesting that a storyboard artist be sent out to the set. The crew was slated to start shooting in two weeks, and there were some key scenes that needed to be worked out. I could only hear one side of the conversation, but it was clear that his need was great and yet they were not about to spend the money to fly someone out to Massachusetts.

I didn't know what a storyboard was, but I did know that it had something to do with drawing and drawing was something I knew about. At dinner that evening I sat next to the production designer thinking about how I would broach the subject, when he turned to me and said, "I want you to know that you can ask me anything." For a second I was shocked, but I recovered enough to take a deep breath and leap into my proposal that the production hire me to work on the storyboards.

He looked surprised and let out a groan, "Oh, no. We just hired someone this afternoon. Too bad, I would have liked to give you a chance. We'll have to catch you on the next one." I was distraught. If only I'd spoken up sooner, I might have been able to stay with the crew and get some great experience. I went back to my hotel room that night and packed my bag. I was due to return to Boston the next morning.

At 6 a.m. the phone rang. I groggily answered it and heard a chipper voice declare, "If you can get over here in 20 minutes with a sharpened pencil, we'll give you a shot. The other artist just backed out." I jumped into my clothes and ran over to the production office. The designer told me that they were about to leave on an all-day location scout and I was to stick close to the director, not ask too many questions, and take notes on everything he said about camera positioning, blocking, and composition.

For the next 14 hours I dutifully followed the many-headed beast that a film crew tends to resemble. I wrote and listened and tried to make sense out of the new vocabulary that was being tossed about. At the end of the day I went back to my room both elated and exhausted. It was the beginning of two months on location and fourteen years of work and study in the art and business of film.

I moved to Los Angeles after finishing the film in the Cape and eventually expanded my experience to include set decoration and art direction. But I always returned to preproduction visualization. I storyboarded, helped directors create shot lists and overhead diagrams, and generally acted as a visual assistant on many feature film and television projects.

In 1990 I was invited to teach a seminar on storyboarding at the American Film Institute. I created a weekend workshop based on my experiences working with first-time directors. These men and women often came to directing through writing and were much less comfortable communicating about the visual aspects of the medium than they were about the narrative. I set out to make visual communication accessible to those filmmakers who felt they had no "talent" for it.

From the beginning, the workshop achieved a popularity neither AFI nor I had anticipated. I added private workshops, held each month at a local hotel. Eventually I was asked to join the film faculty at the Art Center College of Design in Pasadena, California. My experience there working with student filmmakers allowed me to develop a curriculum that encompasses many aspects of previsualization for film, including color theory, composition, storyboarding, and narrative structure as it applies to constructing the frame.

This book is an extension of the work that has come out of those classes as well as others I have given at the Director's Guild of America, the University of Southern California, and the International Filmschool in Cologne, Germany. It has brought me great joy to introduce and expand upon the aesthetic as well as the technical aspects of visualization for film. I hope that the information contained in this volume will be of some use to you in your projects, whether they be for the classic media of film and television or the many varieties of new media (CD-ROMs, the Internet, etc.) that take us beyond linear structure.

Lifeboat 1944

155 154   INT. LIFEBOAT (MORNING) - CLOSE SHOT - THE GERMAN

Struggling with the steering oar to keep the boat from
capsizing, his eyes are on:

1
Introduction

"I think one of the biggest problems that we
have in our business is the inability of people
to visualize. Imagine a composer sittting down
with a blank music sheet in front of him, and a
full orchestra. 'Flute, give me a note if you
please. Yes, thank you very much,' and he
writes it down. It's the same thing, but a man
can compose music directly on paper and
what's the result? It comes out as gorgeous
sounds. The visual, to me, is a vital element in
this work. I don't think it is studied enough."

Alfred Hitchcock, *Directing the Film*

This book is intended for filmmakers such as directors, writers, designers, and cinematographers as well as those in the related fields of art and design who would like to transfer their skills to a new medium. Anyone working in either the traditional arts of film and television or those exploring the new domains of digital video, CD-ROMs and the Internet will find ideas and techniques that will expand their communication skills.

The Details

This book has been broken down into chapters on production, history of the craft, creating a visual shot list, overhead diagramming, and drawing. In addition, one chapter offers ideas about how to express camera movement with the use of frames extended beyond their usual aspect ratio. Another covers the basics of composition with an emphasis on narrative. There is also an illustrated glossary that links words, images, and diagrams for some of the most commonly used terminology in film and video production.

Preproduction visualization is an exciting, demanding process that begins in your imagination and ends with concrete documents that describe your project with imagery. This book will supply you with the tools you need to communicate the visual aspects of your work. You do not need to be an accomplished artist or even feel comfortable about drawing to accomplish this task. While you are learning some simple techniques, this book will lead you on a journey to visual awareness.

Each chapter covers a different aspect of visual communication and how it relates to film and video pre-production. Creating a visually specific shot list, developing an overhead diagram, and expressing your vision through the simple sketching of perspective and figures will be explored in detail. In addition, there are numerous examples of storyboards and other preproduction documents from the history of film and television. The material that is presented strives to be both accessible to the beginner and challenging to the professional.

Why Storyboard?

Film and video are highly collaborative media. Most projects depend on the input and cooperation of dozens if not hundreds of co-workers. In order for the production to work smoothly there needs to be a method to communicate about the numerous decisions that must be made by each department and coordinated by the director and his or her senior staff. The storyboard and its related documents — the shot list and the overhead diagram — are essential tools for communicating visual ideas to the entire crew.

Storyboarding involves logistical as well as aesthetic considerations. Time is money, and time spent planning during preproduction is much cheaper than time spent while the cameras are rolling. Any decisions that can be made prior to principal photography are less expensive decisions than those made on the set. Whether it is a decision regarding the movement of the camera or the blocking of the characters, storyboarding can make your choices clearer from the camera's point of view. From establishing the number of set-ups needed for a stunt or prioritizing your needs for a special effects shot, pre-production visualization brings the crew closer to a unified purpose.

A film or video project is rarely shot without a script. And, just as a screenplay is the script for the narrative of a story, the storyboard is the visual script. Storyboards allow the director time and space to translate the dialogue and action of the screenplay into the language of imagery. When a director first begins the process of visualizing the script, he or she is faced with an unbroken narrative of story line. Contemporary screenwriting style avoids describing camera angles or visual transitions and mainly sticks to describing action and expressing dialogue. The overhead diagram, shot list, and storyboard images are often the first time that the script is translated into imagery. The words of the script may be poetic, but the storyboard is a concrete realization of that poetry into space and time.

Quo Vadis 1951
director Mervyn LeRoy

"Good pre-planning is probably the most important thing, if you want to make a picture within a reasonable budget. If you don't want to waste money, it is very, very important to plan it out. I make little thumbnail sketches all along, and it works. This comes from the animation technique, that is what taught me to make storyboards.

George Pal, *Directing the Film*
director: *The Time Machine*, dozens of animated shorts

The Approach

Storyboarding is often thought of as imagery: minimal sketches that illustrate what the camera will see and how it will move. Our approach will encompass a larger task through the use of a three-tired document made up of:

•**TEXT** (the script and shot list)

•**DIAGRAMS** (overhead schematics)

•**IMAGES** (drawings, photos, computer graphic imagery)

This trilogy of form takes into consideration that the information will be accessible to all manner of minds. Everyone sees things differently. Imagery is concrete; it has a visible connection to the object it signifies. Show a picture of a chair to people unfamiliar with the object and they'll be able to find it in a room immediately. But use the word with people who don't speak English and they won't understand what you're talking about. Words are abstract and leave lots of room open for interpretation. A "follow-shot" of a character can be set up from any number of angles and move in many different ways. We need a language that is broad enough for everyone to understand.

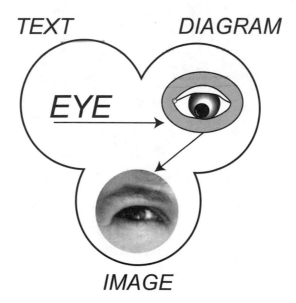

In some ways, the diagram is the best of both worlds. It is both concrete and abstract. It can show where the actors are in relation to the settings and the movement of characters and cameras. Symbols such as arrows and boxes with angles attached can be used to represent blocking and camera positions. The diagram may be the most powerful document of the trilogy, as it can express a large amount of information in a minimal structure.

The connection of these three documents — the image (a drawing or photo-based representation), text (the shot list), and diagram (an overhead of the set with camera positions and character blocking) — assures that anyone reading the preproduction material will get the message. Translating the information into these three languages guarantees that you will be understood.

Through examples culled from the history of film and the writings and interviews of filmmakers, we will explore the ideas — both in words and images — that have influenced the process of envisioning a work and communicating that vision to one's collaborators.

As you work through the information in the book, you may find some of it familiar, while other sections challenge your abilities. Do not be intimidated by the new material. If you're accustomed to dealing with the world on a verbal level, then visual expression will be a stretch. That's OK — muscles that haven't been used for a long time may ache as they are exercised again.

Ivan the Terrible
drawing: Sergei Eisenstein

The Five 'A' s

The five areas covered in the book will significantly affect the way you think about and express yourself regarding visual thought:

- **Assessment** of the script's narrative structure and the translation of story content to visual detail. The conscious use of composition and color can be a powerful story-telling tool. You rarely need to tell the audience what you can show them.

- **Ability** to express vision. Once you have the image in your mind's eye, you need the skill to be able to project and render it onto paper.

- **Attention** to the frame. The perimeters of our visual awareness are defined by the shape and the content of the frame. The chapters on aspect ratio, extended framing, and composition will focus attention in this area.

- **Awareness** of movement. There are two dynamics to this equation: movement of the frame (the camera) and movement inside the frame (the characters and the props).

- **Agreement** between text and image. The shot list and the images that represent its visual content must point to the same decisions. For example, if the shot list says to pan from a profile c/u to an American shot of another character, the image must show that move, that scale, that angle.

How to Use This Book

A final word about the way to use this book. The chapters have been arranged to flow from general information to the specifics of technique. You may want to skim all the chapters briefly and then come back for a closer look once you have a feeling for the structure. Or you can start at the beginning and work your way through each section. Along the way, the words of various directors, designers, illustrators, and other visual thinkers are sprinkled throughout the text to give alternate points of view on the process of visualization.

However you approach the work, remember that you are teaching your mind and your body to see and communicate in a new way. This can be frustrating as well as rewarding. Allow yourself to fail and soon you will find yourself succeeding at a new level of ability. There is often a breakdown before a breakthrough. You may be surprised by the speed of your progress.

Sc. 128 A.
INT. P.B.Y COCK PIT. PILOT & CO-PILOT.
AS THEY HEAD FOR SUB (over shoulder shot.)

Destination Tokyo 1942

Here Comes the Maserati

Occasionally I have been asked to create artworks for characters who
are painters. This artist-for-hire position can be a good fill-in for
the quiet times between features. I've done nudes for Jennifer Jason
Leigh and landscapes for Sally Field. Murals for Korean, Hispanic,
and Japanese painters. And once, an entire outdoor art fair.

The scene called for a group of paintings that had been produced by
various artists, like you would see in a group show. The challenge
was that this art show was to have an unwanted guest -- a fiery red
Maserati, that was to speed through the show, scattering canvases in
its wake. Most rental houses would look unkindly at treating their
artwork in this manner.

The art director asked me to create a total of 42 works in 6
different styles. The scene was scheduled to be shot the next week.
Forty-two paintings in six days. The art department dropped off the
blank canvases on Monday morning and I sat staring at them for a good
long while. I realized what I had committed to and was feeling like
being committed. Then I decided to approach it like a storyboard
assignment. My usual method is to sit down and write up a shot list,
then rough out all the drawings in the morning, spending only 5-7
minutes on each image. Then after lunch, I'll go back into them and
tighten up the drawing, ink them, and add light and shadows.

I started out by making a list of the six different artists' styles I
would attempt to represent. I did faux O'Keeffes, fake Dalis, and
phony Cassats among others. Then I spent an hour priming the canvases
with a few base colors. When that dried, each got a one-hour
treatment in the artist style of the day. They were not good
paintings, but they passed at a distance, and that was the idea.

The canvases were shipped off to the art fair, and I was invited to
be on site when the Maserati made its way through the easels. It was
delicious fun. Most of the paintings were damaged or destroyed during
the several takes needed to shoot the scene. I left as the crew was
shoveling the remains into a dumpster. It's best not to get attached
to the work.

I thought nothing of their fate until years later, when I arrived for
an interview at the production offices of the company that had made
the film. I looked up as I walked into the office and there were the
familiar fakes that I had whipped out in my little West L.A. studio.
Someone had rescued the least damaged ones and taken them back to the
art department. They had been circulating for years on the walls of
the floating production offices. From one show to the next, they had
become part of an unofficial rotating library of art.

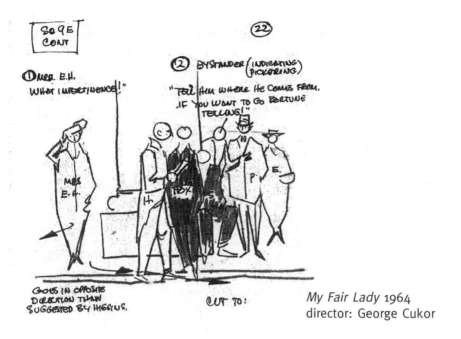

My Fair Lady 1964
director: George Cukor

2 Storyboards in Preproduction

"If George Cukor wanted me to do sketches and work with the cameraman on getting the shots set up, he would do it. On *My Fair Lady* that's the way he had me working with him. That's just the relationship between the director and his production designer. It was ideal. Cukor was a big enough person so that he never felt it was taking anything away from him. His attitude was 'If I can hire him, I can fire him. And if I can fire him I don't worry about him.' "

Gene Allen
production designer: *My Fair Lady*

Storyboards in Preproduction

2

What is a storyboard? The answer may seem self-evident, but the reality is more complex and interesting than just simple, framed drawings. This chapter will cover the definition of storyboards and how they are used in different preproduction processes. Following the journalist's guideline of covering "the five W's" of a story, the information is broken down into **what, why, who, when**, and **where**. These short essays deal with the physical properties of the storyboard — who develops it and who gets to see it down the line, how to prioritize the script in terms of which scenes require boarding first, and when the process usually takes place within the schedule of production.

What kinds of storyboards are used in the various entertainment industries? There is more than one kind of storyboard, and each one has its own style as well as different types of content. This section covers the general attributes of these documents as well as the varied uses they have in filmmaking, television production, commercials, and interactive media.

Why do we use storyboards in preproduction? The dividing line between preproduction and production is the beginning of principal photography. Before the crew and cast are present, making visual decisions can be done in a quieter, more contemplative environment. Once the "troops" arrive, the decision-making can turn more logistic than aesthetic. The "why" of storyboarding concerns itself with both of these factors.

Who creates the storyboard and its related documents? This part of the chapter deals with which crew members are included in the process of creating the visual script as well as who receives the board if the director chooses to circulate it to the crew.

Where and **when** is the storyboard created? This section covers the use of locations, set designs, and scheduling when working on preproduction visualization. The chapter will also include an outline for the storyboard conference — usually a meeting between the director and an illustrator or art director — and how to best use the time to visualize the film frame.

The preproduction process is as varied as the people who work within it. Take this information as it is intended — as a general map of the preproduction process, which changes with each shift of perspective.

FYI: A word on order

You may notice that this list of W's does not follow the proscribed order of **who, what, where, when, why.** That is because in production, you really need to understand What the process is before you determine Who is going to be a part of it and When it is going to happen.

what

why

who

when

where

The Greatest Show on Earth 1952
director: Cecil B. DeMille
drawing: John Jensen

"*The Greatest Show on Earth* didn't have a script or
anything at the time I met DeMille. But he liked to see
visualizations of things. He said, 'I want you to go and
travel with the circus and sketch everything you think
looks interesting.' So I traveled with the circus and
lived with them on the circus train. I stayed with them
a couple of months. And later on, after I'd been sketching up these scenes a while, he'd have the writers
write the story around these sketches."

John Jensen
illustrator: *The Greatest Show on Earth*

What is a Storyboard?

The use of the storyboard, as well as the shot list and overhead diagram, is widespread in many fields of the entertainment industry. Commercials, industrial films, CD-ROMs, and Web sites all use some form of storyboarding to help plan out the relationship of images to other aspects of the project.

Different media and the various artists and technicians who work in them have different needs and use different types of boards. The following pages will plot out basic styles and the uses that storyboards have within the various industries.

Storyboards can be referred to as:

- **Editorial Storyboards**

- **Key Frames**

- **Production Illustrations**

- **Commercial Boards**

"In silent films we didn't have all the words to explain everything, we thought in terms of symbols, graphic arrangements, or possibilities. We were trained in these terms. When you had to explain something you didn't think, 'What's the exact word for this? The exact phrase or sentence?' You just thought, 'What's the picture, the symbol?' "

King Vidor, *Directing the Film* director: *The Crowd, Our Daily Bread*

Editorial Storyboarding

There are a few types of storyboards, but we will only cover one of these in detail in this book. The film and television industries use the Editorial method to give visual expression to the flow of edited sequences from the screenplay. These images are most often characterized by quick black-and-white sketches and can be simple line drawings or complex renderings of light and shadow.

- **Plots out the editorial sequencing (how the shots will be edited, not the order of shooting)**

- **Reflects the creative concepts of the Director**

- **8 1/2" by 11" format, usually for one to four frames per page**

- **Black and White**

- **Quick Sketch**

The editorial storyboard is a Xerox art form in the sense that in most cases, the crew rarely works off the original storyboards. Instead, Xeroxes are made of the originals and then distributed to the crew. The storyboards need to be high-contrast so they will reproduce well, so black-and-white storyboards are standard. In special circumstances, a Saturday matinee-type movie such as *Indiana Jones and the Raiders of the Lost Ark* will be rendered in color. High-style productions can benefit from adding color in the early stages of preproduction visualization, and obviously, movies with that kind of budget can afford the luxury of this more time-demanding process. What's more, the color drawings are then also available for any book that may be published on the making of the film, or as a special feature when the movie is released on DVD.

Storyboards come in a variety of formats. Most productions make do with black-and-white sketches that focus on camera angle and composition. The drawings are often rendered on an 8 1/2" by 11" page that is easily integrated into the script. Some directors feel that working with only one image per page gives them the freedom to manipulate individual storyboard frames into alternate sequences. Other filmmakers ask for little more than thumbnail drawings, small renditions of frames that can have up to a dozen or more stacked onto a page. The size of these frames is solely up to the director's discretion.

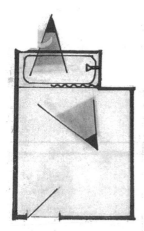

SC. 173 - SHOOTING OVER BATHTUB AS THORNDYKE ENTE

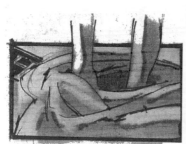

AS ROBE DROPS TO THE FLOOR....

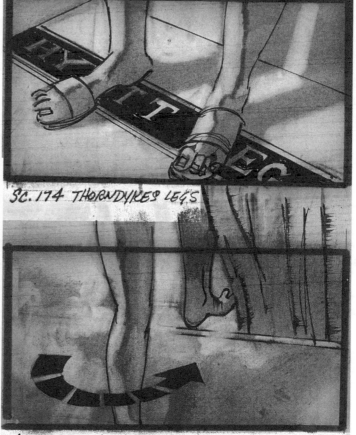

SC. 174 THORNDYKE'S LEGS

HE TURNS AND ENTERS TUB AS WE

High Anxiety 1977
director: Mel Brooks
drawing: Harold Michelson

17

The Key Frame

- **More highly rendered than an editorial board**
- **Only shows highlight images from the sequence**
- **Often used as a sales tool**
- **Generally, one image per page on an 8 1/2" by 11" paper**

There are times when a full editorial treatment is unwanted or unnecessary. In that case, key frames might be an appropriate substitution. Key frames pick out important moments in the story and elaborately render them, using a highly developed level of light and shadow. These frames are sometimes utilized when a producer or director is still attempting to raise money for a specific production. These drawings can act as sales tools to give the investors or studios a simple visualization of some of the proposed project's most prominent scenes. It is important to note that these drawings often fall short of being full-scale production illustrations (see below). They are meant to suggest a mood and style rather than communicate steadfast decisions. In fact, there can be a danger in showing up to a pitch meeting with too much polish on the material.

"I worked on *The Towering Inferno* as a conceptual artist and storyboarder. I boarded shots for four different camera crews. They had the stars working every day and they also had a miniature unit and a helicopter unit, and everyone had to know what everyone else was doing. The action stuff was dictated by the special effects angles chosen by the director on the miniatures. I would run back and forth between the crews and Irwin Allen, the director, says, 'Just stay ahead of me Joe, just stay ahead.' "

Joseph Musso
illustrator: *The Towering Inferno, Torn Curtain, Volcano*

Volcano 1997
director: Mick Jackson
drawings: Joseph Musso

Production Illustration

- **Used to fully render lighting**

- **Highly detailed and polished**

- **Always a wide shot of the set**

- **Reflects the creative concepts of the Production Designer**

- **Used as a tool for the designer to sell set design ideas to the director and producer**

- **Large scale, perhaps 14" by 20" or more, one image per paper**

The production illustration is a polished and highly detailed, fully realized image that depicts the setting either at a dramatic moment or without characters, as the set might be seen in an establishing shot.

There are vast sums of money devoted to the design of the settings for each production. Unless you are going to shoot at primarily existing locations, each set needs to be designed and then signed off on by the director and some combination of producers. Often, a model is built for each set. The model can either be a white version that shows only the basic structures or a fully painted maquette that features color, texture, and furnishings. Either way, the model focuses on space.

In addition to this model, many designers use production illustrations that show the set from a wide-angle view that might or might not be part of the actual shot continuity. The purpose of this drawing is twofold: One is to give a sense, in two-dimensions, of the appearance of the set. The other is to give the designer an opportunity to express his or her ideas on how the set might be lit.

> "I also sketch most of the sets, production illustrations with quick shadows. The drawings can get expressionistic, but I try and be good, to stay with reality. I start with something quick, to get across an idea, then we focus in and I redraw and get more specific. On the major sets we also did models."

Richard Hoover
production designer: *Girl, Interrupted*

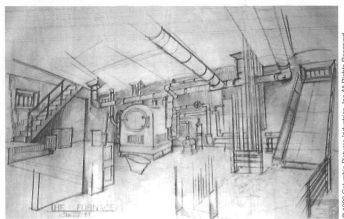

Girl, Interrupted 1999
director: James Mangold
drawing: Richard Hoover

Commercial Storyboards
(Also called Comps)

- **Highly rendered color images of the commercial spot**

- **Reflects the creative concepts of the Advertising Agency**

- **Used as a sales tool to present ideas to the client**

- **No camera moves shown**

- **Standard frame up to 6" by 8," mounted on a board in sequence**

The commercial world bears little resemblance to feature films or broadcast television as far as the use of storyboards in the initial stages of preproduction. Commercials are usually envisioned by advertising agencies, not the people who will eventually direct them. Therefore, the first storyboard is a sales tool that is commissioned by the client (i.e., a car manufacturer) and then drawn up by the agency to show their ideas on the proposed spot. Once approved, this board is then used to get directors and production companies to bid on the commercial. Once the job has been awarded, the director then has the option to create his or her own shooting boards for the spot that follow the agency's editorial storyboard structure.

Flying Bros
drawing: John Dahlstrom

Materials Used for the Editorial Storyboard

Artists use a wide variety of materials when creating an editorial storyboard, ranging from a simple pencil to a state-of-the-art computer system. Most artists still employ the classic techniques of a light, rough under-sketch and then a polish level of black lines and gray-tone shadows. The materials used can include non-photo blue pencils for the under-drawing, and graphite pencils ranging from the soft, 4B variety to harder ones up to 2H for the bulk of sketching. Also, colored pencils that have a waxy content (like Prismacolor or Verithin brands) produce good, dark lines for the over-drawing details. Some artists love to add shadows with a cotton swab dipped in powdered graphite. It quickly covers large areas of the drawing, and then light can be added in by dragging an eraser over the gray-tone areas. Some artists sketch with pencil and then detail the drawing with a variety of pens and markers. These materials are less forgiving, as it is more difficult to erase or lighten-up an area that has gone too dark.

Other materials that have been used in older examples of storyboards include colored pastels, gouache, watercolor, and charcoal. These materials are very beautiful in their many applications, and if you have the time, they will reward your investigations. But beware the surface — charcoal and pastel will spread and smear, so you will need to protect your originals with a fixative and/or cover sheet.

One technique I have enjoyed starts off with sketching a simple sketch with a graphite pencil on white bond paper. I make all my overall decisions on composition and framing in this first step. Then I will make a couple of copies of the drawing onto a heavier paper and use those versions to play around with light, shadow, and maybe color, if the situation calls for it. The final version is then re-Xeroxed and handed out to the appropriate crew members. This technique is time-consuming and usually used with the type of board discussed below.

Materials Used in Key Frame Sketches

Because of their use as sales tools, key frames are often rendered in color. Artists use a great variety of media for color sketches, including, but not limited to: colored pencil, pastel, watercolor, markers, pen, and charcoal. Because the key frame deals with individual setups instead of sequences, it is often rendered one to a page in the 8 1/2" by 11" format, or larger, if desired by the director or the producer.

Choosing your Materials

A description of the materials commonly used in the development of each type of board previously described is listed below. This list is only meant as a guide to your creativity. There is no correct single way to render these images. In the end, the choice of material is one that is ruled by the senses, not the intellect. Paper has a particular feel to it: smooth, rough, reflective, matte. Pencils offer a great number of qualities: hard or soft, waxy or chalky. These choices come down to personal preferences. Spend a while in an art supply store and test drive some of the materials. If you are just beginning to collect some supplies, buy a variety of pencils and see which of them responds best to your touch. Experiment. Enjoy.

The lists are by no means comprehensive, as every artist, director, or designer experiments and finds a technique that is most comfortable for her or him. This is just a general guide for those readers who may need to visit an art supply store before starting on a new project.

EDITORIAL STORYBOARDS
8.5" by 11" paper
non-photo blue pencil
graphite pencils, HB, 2B
Black pens (try Penstix, in a variety of
  widths: F, EF, EEF)
Prismacolor pencil: Black
Verithin pencil: Indigo
Sharpener
Kneaded eraser
Triangle: 90 degree with a hypotenuse
  of at least 12"

PRODUCTION ILLUSTRATIONS
Full sheets of paper 20" by 30" or
  illustration board
A set of gouache paints, brushes
Set of colored pencils
Graphite pencils
Toned markers
Variety of black pens

COMMERCIAL COMPS
Marker paper, 11" by 14"
Full sets of color and gray tone
  markers
Non-photo blue pencil
Graphite pencils
Variety of black pens
Black board for mounting

KEY FRAMES
8.5" by 11" paper, or larger
  As these can be color or B&W,
  follow the lists for editorial boards or
  production illustration

Materials Used in Production Illustration

Designers use a wide variety of media for this kind of sketch, including pencil, pen, pastel, charcoal, and gouache. The size of the illustrations can vary, but they are usually much larger than a typical storyboard frame — up to 20" by 30". They are typically rendered on a good sheet of illustration board or pastel paper.

Materials Used in Commercial Boards

Commercial boards are almost always full-color renderings. They are formatted using the television aspect ratio of 1:1.33 and are most often drawn with a set of toned markers. The boards only show composition, not camera movement. Also, the voiceover and dialogue track are inserted in a box below the image. These are highly polished images, down to the glint of light on a car's fender. They are, above all, about selling visual ideas to a client.

An Overview

How do these four applications of preproduction visualization relate to each other?

- The **editorial board** plans out all the shots in a film to tell the story, scene by scene. The shots are then arranged in editorial sequence so that the director and the crew can refer to them during filming.

- The **key frames** only show a selection of shots, perhaps only crucial sequences or the most complex camera moves, or the establishing shot at the beginning of the scene.

- The **production illustration** isn't really a storyboard in that it focuses on showing a set rather than a shot. It is generally created by the production designer rather than the director.

- The **commercial board** is a sales tool typically used by an advertising agency to present a concept to a client. It is often created before the director is even hired for the spot.

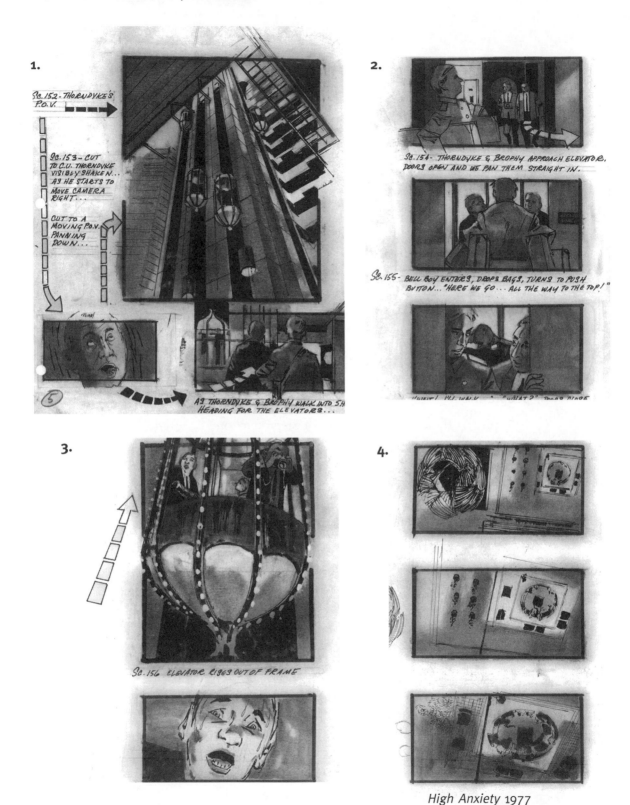

1.

Sc.152-THORNDYKE'S P.O.V.

Sc.153 - CUT TO C.U. THORNDYKE VISIBLY SHAKEN... AS HE STARTS TO MOVE CAMERA RIGHT...

CUT TO A MOVING P.O.V. PANNING DOWN...

AS THORNDYKE & BROPHY WALK INTO SH HEADING FOR THE ELEVATORS...

2.

Sc.154- THORNDYKE & BROPHY APPROACH ELEVATOR. DOORS OPEN AND WE PAN THEM STRAIGHT IN.

Sc.155- BELL BOY ENTERS, DROPS BAGS, TURNS TO PUSH BUTTON..."HERE WE GO...ALL THE WAY TO THE TOP!"

3.

Sc.156 ELEVATOR RISES OUT OF FRAME

4.

High Anxiety 1977
director: Mel Brooks
drawings: Harold Michelson

24

Case Study

High Anxiety

"I sat down with Hitchcock a few times when I had done a sequence that I thought was terrific. He looked at it and he said, 'This is really terrific, but I can't use it here.' And I thought, he's jealous. You know what I mean? But he was absolutely right because not only couldn't he use it, but also he explained why. A lot of people miss out because they're thinking of great shots and they lose sight of the story. And the story is a symphony that builds up to a certain thing, and this is not the place to put this absolutely sensational sequence. I was concentrating on my storyboard, which was going to be the best damn storyboard that you ever saw, except you couldn't use it there."

Harold Michelson
illustrator: *High Anxiety, The Birds, The Graduate*

5.

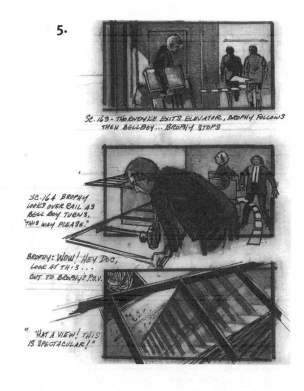

6.

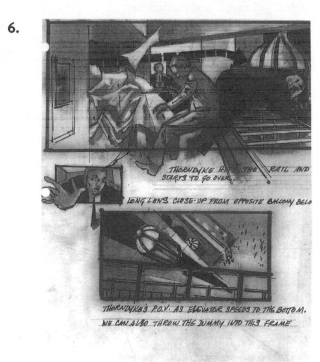

"I hate the idea of going onto a location or a set someplace and [saying] 'Well, let's see, I wonder where we should put the camera?' I want to be able to say, 'The camera's going to go here, she's going to walk in the door there, and we're going to dolly with her, move in, go over there, and end up with a two-shot of her standing at the desk.' "

Robert Wise

West Side Story 1961
director: Robert Wise
production design: Boris Levin

Editorial Boards: The Focus of this Book

These different techniques all have their place in preproduction, but it is beyond the scope of this book to cover all of them in depth. Certainly, the skills outlined in the following chapters can be applied to any of these endeavors, but this volume will focus on the various aspects of editorial storyboarding for film and television and the relationship storyboards have to the broader process of production.

Why focus on one application? Because the editorial storyboard is the document that is most engaged with the story arc of the script. The intended audience for this information is a mixed group, made up of both filmmakers who may have limited drawing skills and artists who have a limited knowledge of film production. The editorial board, with its heavy emphasis on camera placement and character blocking as well as the sequence of shots telling the story, gives both the director and the designer a wide margin for input and collaboration.

What to Storyboard? Prioritzing the Scenes

When you are preparing a script for a feature film there are situations when you have less than enough time to storyboard the entire script. You may have a modest budget that will allow you to work with a professional illustrator for only two weeks. That kind of time frame lets you visualize a few major scenes, but not much more than that. You need to prioritize the scenes to ensure that the most demanding of them will be worked out within the time and space your particular circumstance allows.

The paragraphs below cover the types of scenes that are most often storyboarded in preparation for the shoot. Some productions have the time and money to treat each scene to a thorough visualization. If you are working on a science fiction film, an action series, or a screen translation of a comic book, you may find that you have the time and budget to work on a complete visual script.

The list below is for those projects that need to concentrate their resources and storyboard a select group of scenes.

- **Special effects shots (a.k.a. FX or EFX)**
- **Stunts and pyrotechnics**
- **Crowd scenes**
- **Action**
- **Complex camera movements**
- **Montage sequences**
- **Opening and closing scenes**

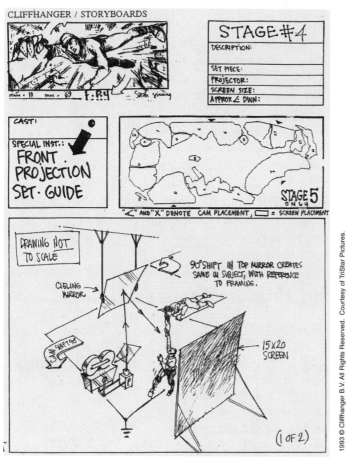

1. Special effects or FX shots are virtually always storyboarded. Most production companies do not have the internal resources to create FX shots in-house. That means that in each circumstance the work will have to be contracted out to an effects house. In order for the company to understand the production's needs, some visualization should accompany the script pages with the request for a bid on the job.

Cliffhanger 1993
director: Renny Harlin
drawings: John Mann

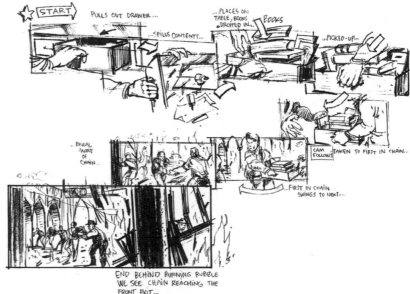

Ten Commandments 1956
director: Cecil B. DeMille
drawing: Harold Michelson

Many special effects houses have their own artists who work on visualization of the shots in question. They can work in the traditional mediums of pencil, charcoal, or marker on paper, or use advanced computer software that allows the shot to be real-ized in the "three dimensions" of a virtual world. Either way, the conversation between the production company, the direc-tor, and the effects group will take place as much in the visual sphere of communication as in the verbal one.

2. Stunts and pyrotechnics are the next types of situations that will require storyboard attention. These shots are heavily choreographed and often can only be acted out one time because of cost, availability of materials, and danger to those involved. Also, multiple cameras are used in many of these cases, and the director and cinematographer will want to have as much input as possible for these second unit crews.

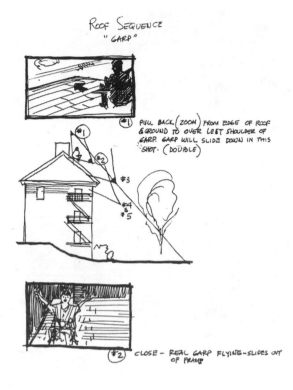

ROOF SEQUENCE
"GARP"

#1 PULL BACK (ZOOM) FROM EDGE OF ROOF & GROUND TO OVER LEFT SHOULDER OF GARP. GARP WILL SLIDE DOWN IN THIS SHOT. (DOUBLE)

#2 CLOSE - REAL GARP FLYING - SLIDES OUT OF FRAME

#3 LONGER ANGLE - REAL GARP - SLIDING INTO CAMERA.

REAL GARP & DOUBLE SLIDES OF ROOF LEFT LEG GOES THRU GUTTER.

GARP ROLLS OVER ON STOMACH & TRIES TO CATCH CORNICE

GARP ON STOMACH... TRYING TO HOLD ON.

The World According to Garp 1982
director: George Roy Hill

3. Crowd scenes are a good bet for the production that has a limited storyboarding budget. A crowd can consist of 20 or 2,000 people. At either extreme it is often useful to have a set of storyboards to hand out to a crew that may be more than taxed with the overload of bodies on the set. It is also another situation where multiple cameras may be utilized. If these sequences have already been boarded out, the director, assistant directors, and other crew members will have one less element to think about during a challenging day on the set.

Quo Vadis 1951
director: Mervyn LeRoy

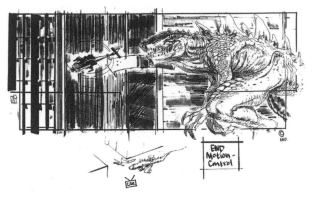

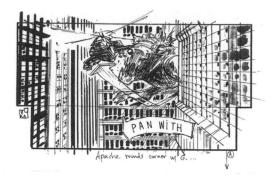

4. Action sequences, such as staged fights and car chases, lend themselves to storyboarding because they are usually highly choreographed, and therefore need to be visualized in great detail before the cameras roll. If an illustrator can be included in the rehearsals of the fight action, then the director will have a good visual record of the shot possibilities of that scene. Sometimes all that is necessary is a 35mm camera with a zoom or a video camera to block out the camera positions. That visual information can then be worked with to create a plan of action for photographing the action scene.

Godzilla 1998
director: Roland Emmerich
drawings: John Mann

5. Complex camera movement is another type of shot that lends itself to storyboarding. In the case of extended crane moves, handheld, or steadicam shots, the use of overhead diagrams tied in with sketches of frame compositions can cut down rehearsal time drastically. Or they can serve as a starting point for discussions about the shot. Either way, these visual tools encourage conversation and expedite communication.

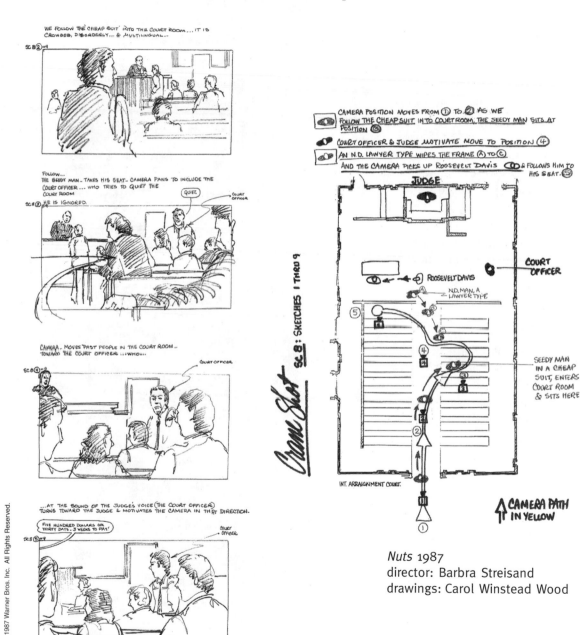

Nuts 1987
director: Barbra Streisand
drawings: Carol Winstead Wood

6. Montage sequences have a specialized meaning in American filmmaking. The word montage was originally used by European filmmakers to mean editing in general. In the United States we have narrowed the term to apply to sequences that are edited with highly compressed time and space and usually have no dialogue. A popular example of this can be found in the shopping sequence in *Pretty Woman*, when Julia Roberts's character goes on a whirlwind tour of the best stores in Los Angeles, backed up by an instrumental rendition of the title song. An all-day expedition is related in a three-minute collage of images that edits six hours into three minutes of screen time.

Montage sequences often appear in the written script as no more than a sentence or two that instructs the director to describe a passage of time using a whirlwind of images and little or no dialogue.

The director and crew must flesh out this shot-heavy sequence visually; the storyboards, shot list, and overhead diagrams are both individually and collectively strong starting points for conversations of this type.

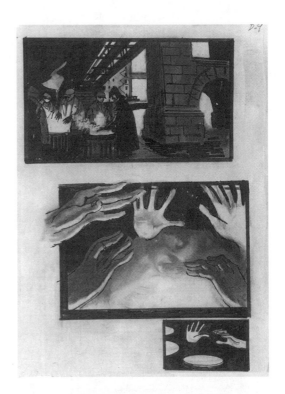

The Cotton Club 1984
director: Francis Coppola
drawings: Harold Michelson

7. Opening and closing sequences can also benefit from the treatment of preproduction visualization. Whether you are working on a feature-length film or a 20-minute industrial, the opening shots of a film strive to pull the audience into its particular world. The style of the film's imagery as well as the feel of its characters can be projected in those first few moments. A clear image of the shots that will make up this sequence can set the tone for the way the entire film is visualized. The same idea can apply to the closing scene of the film. If not a climactic moment, it is a denouement to the full three-act structure, and the imagery of these last moments will stay with the audience long after they leave the theater or turn off their televisions.

8. The Rest. There are no definite rights or wrongs here. This list is meant as a guide to get you started on the scenes that have the most pressing logistic need for the work. In terms of aesthetic needs, anything and everything or nothing at all can be planned in advance. The choice simply has to do with the style and the content of your individual project.

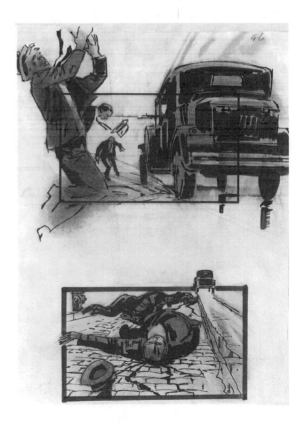

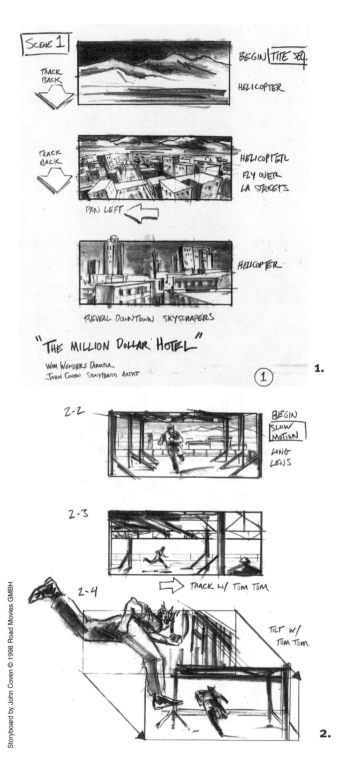

Case Study

The Million Dollar Hotel

"The challenge of storyboarding is representing four dimensions in two. You are representing height, width, and depth on a piece of paper that only has height and width. The dimension that you have in film that you don't have in illustration is time. That is the fourth dimension. The art of story-boarding is in choosing the right moment of time for illustration. You have one frame and you must be able to take one frozen moment from that entire shot and represent it in one or two frames. You need to be able to communicate the entire shot in that one image.

"Each shot gives the audience one piece of information. The question for me as an illustrator is how I communicate that small portion of time through a single image. My background as a children's book Illustrator has helped me concentrate on this aspect of storyboarding."

John Coven
illustrator: *X-Men, The Usual Suspects*

The Million Dollar Hotel 2001
director: Wim Wenders
drawings: John Coven

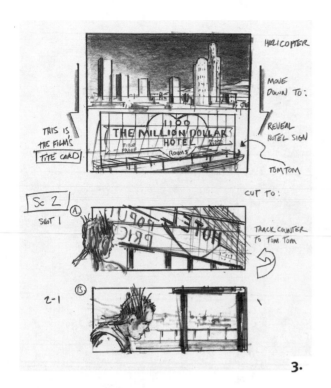

THIS IS THE FILM'S TITE CARD

HELICOPTER

MOVE DOWN TO:

REVEAL HOTEL SIGN

TOM TOM

CUT TO:

Sc 2 SHOT 1 Ⓐ

TRACK COUNTER TO TOM TOM

2-1 Ⓑ

3.

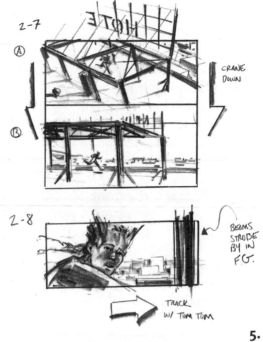

2-7

Ⓐ

Ⓑ

CRANE DOWN

2-8

BEAMS STRODE BY IN F.G.

TRACK W/ TOM TOM

5.

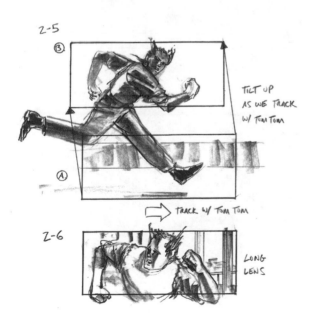

2-5

Ⓑ

TILT UP AS WE TRACK W/ TOM TOM

Ⓐ

TRACK W/ TOM TOM

2-6

LONG LENS

4.

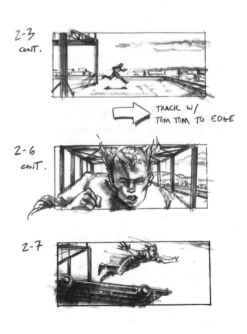

2-3 CONT.

TRACK W/ TOM TOM TO EDGE

2-6 CONT.

2-7

6.

Case Study

Godzilla

"I usually start working in pre-production about two to three months before photography. The larger sized pictures, a hundred million and up, are often very effects driven. They need to board many, many shots in order to get the picture made. So the big pictures will storyboard three-quarters or more of the film. The smaller film might only board a quarter of the movie, the action sequences and so on.

Sometimes you need to create this 'Rube Goldberg' of a storyboard page. It becomes a machine that you are drawing out, a dynamic operation and that takes a lot of time. On a film like Godzilla they expected between 10 to 20 frames a day. And that was with a high degree of polish. I've done other projects where I might whip out up to sixty drawings in a single day and night. But I told the director that they were not going to be pretty drawings."

John Mann
illustrator: *Godzilla*

CHOPPER
ENTERS @ END of MOVE.

"I don't know..."

"...we go through everything scene by scene. I'm really meticulous about this. It's a part of choices that you make in terms of composition, lighting, and staging. What I like to do is talk about the big picture. I write these incredibly long memos about the full vision of the film. It gives the visual department a step-by-step idea of where the character starts, what's the point of view, how that point of view evolves, and what the conclusion is in the end. When a prop guy asks, 'What kind of drinking glass should I get - one with Miss Piggy on it, or should I get the Pyrex kind?' he has been let in on the bigger picture of the film so that we can make the choice in a way that is more realistic."

Jodi Foster
director: LIttle Man Tate,
Home for the Holidays

The Storyboarding Meeting: Who Is Involved?

How many artists does it take to concoct a board? The answer is as individual as each director's taste. Some directors, such as Martin Scorsese and Werner Fassbinder, prefer to work on their own, sketching small images to be used as personal notes during production. Others draw up rough sketches themselves and then hand the drawings over to a skilled illustrator to polish them up before distributing them to the crew. George Roy Hill worked in this way on *The World According to Garp* and *The Great Waldo Pepper.*

Still others like to use their designers or illustrators as visual assistants and work out the shot list and camera positions with them. Then, artists take these notes and translate them into storyboards based on these conversations. And some directors will hand over scenes without much input at all and allow the collaborator to visualize the sequence. Once the storyboard is finished, the director will edit the images and perhaps ask for revisions.

I have worked with directors at both ends of the "input spectrum," from those who stood over my shoulder expressly manipulating the angle and composition of each shot to those who handed over a script and told me to come back in a few days with a few scenes boarded out. The majority fall somewhere between the extremes, feeling comfortable with giving suggestions, but not feeling that they had to control the entire enterprise.

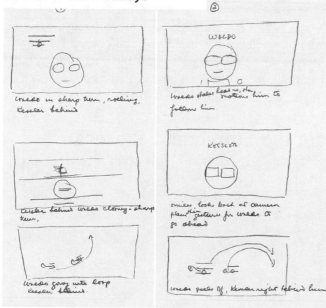

The Great Waldo Pepper 1975
director: George Roy Hill
drawings: George Roy Hill

If I were given a choice, I would like a director to bring an overhead diagram to our storyboard meeting. The diagram includes both abstract and concrete information and is extremely useful to someone trying to visualize the composition of each shot on the list. Some directors will bring in an overhead diagram with actors' movements already worked out. Sometimes there is the time, money, and inclination to rehearse extensively before principal photography. Other times the storyboarding process itself is the extent of the preproduction work on some scenes.

If a director comes to a meeting with one of the three visualization documents already developed, the visual assistant will

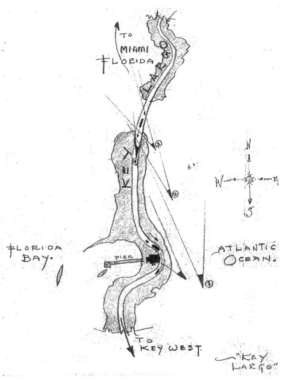

Key Largo 1948

then help to expand that work into a more complete document for the crew. I have gotten up with directors and acted out the scenes with them as we blocked the characters. I have had discussions about motivation of camera moves and the logistics of moving around small locations. The storyboard artist needs to be knowledgeable in editing and composition as well as illustration. The needs of the director vary enormously from project to project, and only by being fluent in the many facets of filmmaking will a visual assistant be able to effectively communicate in the necessary language of the moment

When and Where to Begin the Storyboard Process

The attitude toward this aspect of the process varies from director to director. Some find that drawing and diagramming very early in the process helps them to begin solidifying their ideas about the film. Others prefer to wait until the locations have been locked down and the sets designed before they begin this type of planning.

Visualization
Timeline Chart

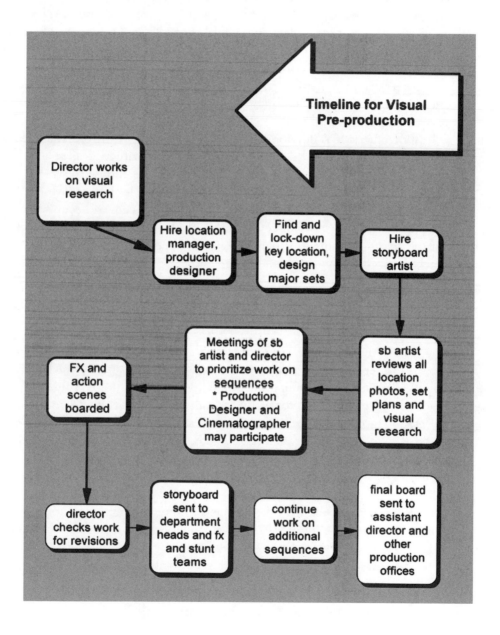

Timeline for Visual Pre-production

Director works on visual research

Hire location manager, production designer

Find and lock-down key location, design major sets

Hire storyboard artist

sb artist reviews all location photos, set plans and visual research

Meetings of sb artist and director to prioritize work on sequences
* Production Designer and Cinematographer may participate

FX and action scenes boarded

director checks work for revisions

storyboard sent to department heads and fx and stunt teams

continue work on additional sequences

final board sent to assistant director and other production offices

Use of Research Materials

When working in collaboration it is important for a director to share his or her visual sources with whoever is brought into the process. Clips from films, magazine pages, and books on art and photography all aid in the communication of a general style or individual shots. If there is time, watch films together and discuss the influence of different sequences, camera angles, and lighting schemes in terms of the project at hand. Often this topic is only discussed between the cinematographer and the director, but opening up the discussion to include the illustrator and the other visual collaborators can allow the crew to be more aligned with the director's vision.

Once the style is developed and understood by all involved, the director can sit down alone or with a partner and begin to clarify ideas in specific images, shot lists, and overhead diagrams. Some people choose to work from images into words, others start with the shot list, then look at an overhead of the set and then place the camera in the positions it needs to occupy in order to cover the action. Other directors start with the overhead diagram, block out the actors' movements first, and then place the camera in position to watch the scene play out.

Locations and Sets: Timing Storyboard Process to Real Space

There are times when the production schedule is so rushed that the process of preparing the visual documents is left to the last two weeks or even the last few days of preproduction. This scenario is not terrific for anyone involved. The director is usually overwhelmed by other demands of the production. Location scouting for new sets, actor rehearsals, meetings with the cinematographer, even last-minute casting decisions demand the director's time. This means that end-run decision making is often done by the supporting staff (i.e., the assistant) and then looked over and approved or changed by the director on the fly.

Now, some people work best under pressure, but my suggestion is that if you have some of the locations identified and a few sets designed early in the process (say, one to two months before shooting), then waste no time and get to the task. Aesthetic decisions made in a calm state of mind are likely to be

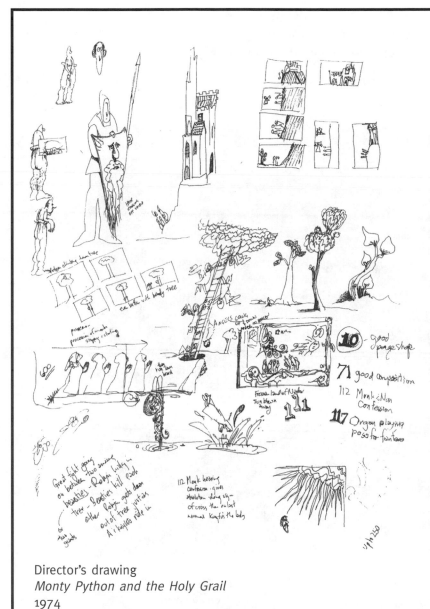

Director's drawing
Monty Python and the Holy Grail
1974

"I can't not draw stuff and I can't not say it should be done this way. But it's a collaborative thing. I have very specific ideas and either I draw them or I drag in references and say 'I want you to look at this.' But, if you get good people, they can interpret this and make it work.... I like working with good people because if I come up with an idea, they come up with a better idea, then I come up with an even better one, and so on: it's a leapfrog process, and the work becomes much better than it would be if only I did exactly what I want."

Terry Gilliam
Gilliam on Gilliam
1999

more true to your artistic sensibility than those made in the heat of pressure. And even if this isn't true for your style of creativity, you can always change your mind about the storyboard as you get closer to the shooting day. It is good to know that you have at least one draft of the visual script available.

Altered location photographs
Ben Hur 1959
director: William Wyler
art director: Ed Carfagno

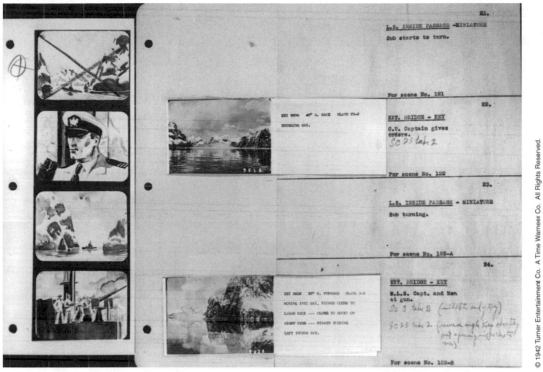

Destination: Tokyo 1943
director: Delmar Daves

Working On Location

• Tools: digital still or video camera
• Floor plans drawn to scale and reduced for easy in-
  script use
• Sketch artist to create visual record of rehearsals

As an artist and visual collaborator, I enjoy
coming onto a production early enough to spend time
with the director and begin to understand his or her
style and conceptual approach to the script. That way,
any design ideas that I incorporate into the storyboards
are more likely to be well-matched to the film's overall
design.

Case Study

Sister, Sister

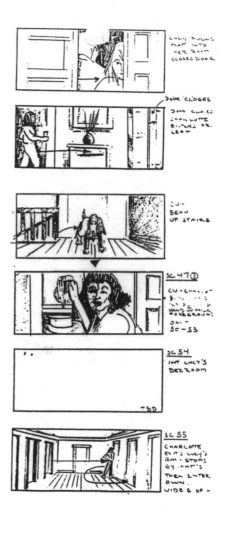

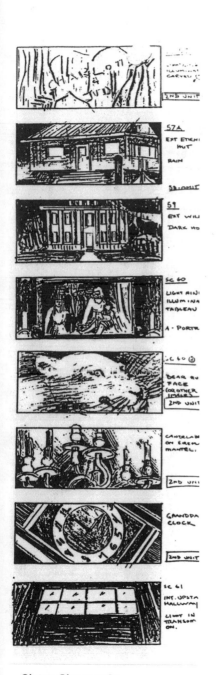

Sister Sister 1987
director: Bill Condon
drawings: Marcie Begleiter

In 1985 I worked with a writer who was preparing to shoot his first feature as director. The producer on this film was an experienced hand who realized that the more input the young director received in terms of story visualization, the better off the production would be when it came to shooting and editing the footage. I was hired on two months before principal photography was to begin. We spent the first week in a screening room viewing films that had influenced the director regarding the style of the project. The script was of the gothic-suspense genre and took place in the sweltering backwoods of Louisiana.

We immersed ourselves in the work of Hitchcock, Robert Aldrich, and Fritz Lang, not to mention books on photography and painting that related to the setting and period of the story. I began to draw the first scene: a lyrical, dreamlike montage of images. The director and producer approved these first efforts and within two weeks we were on our way down to Louisiana to finish the bulk of preproduction on location.

There were four of us in the team; the director, the cinematographer, the production designer, and myself, the storyboard artist. We walked through every location and talked through the scenes shot by shot. I kept notes, took photographs, and participated in the discussions that ranged from general ideas about the color scheme to specific decisions regarding the placement of the camera. By the end of three weeks we had completed the essential scene work, and I continued to draw up the storyboard images that were the visual notes of these meetings. By the time the crew arrived and started preparing for the shoot, we had the majority of the script worked out in a shot list and storyboard frames.

The producer and the director then made an unusual and very interesting request. I was asked to take the storyboards and reduce all the images on an office Xerox machine so that they could be handed out in a condensed form. I had been working on the scenes in editorial order, but the production wanted to hand out copies of the boards to the heads of all the crews, and requested the images in shooting order, with the shots for a day's work on a single sheet.

This handout elicited unexpected comments from my coworkers. The sound technician thanked me for the information. He said it let him plan ahead for what would be required. "Now I've got an idea of which boom to carry into the swamp tonight," he said with grateful amusement. It was a hard shoot, with lots of night work and a fairly unforgiving schedule. I was around for the first two weeks of shooting—one of the characters in the film was a painter and I had been hired to create a series of canvases for her character— and was delighted to see the director walk onto the set each day with the storyboard sheet sticking out of his back pocket.

Months later when I went to see the completed film at the cast and crew screening, I was amazed to find that watching the movie was like seeing the story-board come to life. There was approximately an 80-90% correlation between the boards and the film as it was shot and edited. To this day I feel that this was one of the high points in my experiences as a film collabora-tor. And I credit the experience to the producer, who had the foresight to spend a little extra up-front so that the work of visualizing the film was a priority. The storyboard in that production was a document that came out of a true collaboration of the director, designers, cinematographer, and illustrator.

"I never make story-boards, designs. In fact, I write out my own scenes and then, in the moment of shooting, I really do the opposite of what I have written, generally speaking."

Bernardo Bertoluccim, *Directing the Film*

Ten Commandments 1956
director: Cecil B. DeMille
drawings: Harold Michelson

From The General to the Specific

The information in this chapter has been intended as a general guide to the process of preproduction visualization. The chapters that follow will cover the specifics of creating the storyboard, the shot list, and the overhead diagram. The information needed to create them will be explained in detail and exercises will be offered to focus and develop your visual communication skills.

Points to remember:
- Prioritize your scenes
- Decide on the crew members to be involved with the pre-viz
- Start well ahead of shooting schedule
- Work off of location overheads and floor plans of the set whenever possible
- Determine who will receive the boards and distribute

The Fifth Element
Effects Drawings by Ron Gress

• preliminary drawing

• 3-D digital storyboard

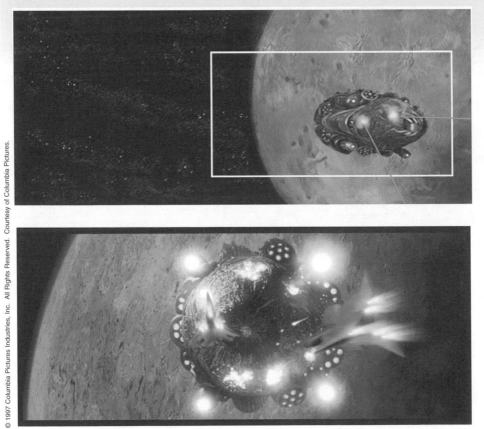

• film frame

The Fifth Element 1997
director: Luc Besson
drawings: Ron Gress

Interview with Ron Gress

My title is Visual Effects Art Director here at Digital Domain [an efx house in Los Angeles]. I primarily develop ideas on the computer in 3-D programs like Bryce 4, Photoshop, and Poser. I also create animatics and make quick-time movies to illustrate the shots for those directors who need help visualizing what they want. So the more complete storyboard you can provide for them the better. I'll take drawings and flesh them out in 2-D and 3-D software. These are my equivalents of storyboards, but they're basically key frame illustrations. They will carry you through a live-action sequence.

At Digital Domain we are often approached by directors who bring us a script and ask us to identify which elements need digital effects, or sometimes they come to us with key frames and ask us to flesh them out. It depends on how active the production designer and the director are together on planning the digital effects. Many directors lack experience in that area and they leave it to the visual effects supervisor. The job is relatively new, it's just been used for the last few years, and the visual effects art director is even newer. I acquired that title for myself a few years ago when I was brought onto *The Fifth Element*.

On a picture like that there might be five key people working on a single sequence. One working on the camera move, someone else working on the models, another working on the lighting, and another on the 2D and 3-D elements. Then we have a leader who oversees everyone and acts as an administrator. The hierarchy might look like this: the Visual Effects Supervisor over the Digital Effects Supervisor and then the Art Directors reporting to them, just like any other film crew. Then there is — on top of all that — the executive producer, who has the final say.

Sometimes the director might like to talk to me rather than filter the information through someone else. Once I've done the still frames or an animatic I'll take it to the Visual Effects Supervisor who will give me feedback, and then the material goes to the artists again, version through version. Sometimes there might be 50 or 60 iterations of a visual effect before it finally gets approved by the director in the screening room.

It's Two in the Morning.....

I was working as a set decorator on a non-union feature.
It was Friday, and since there was no turnaround time
minimum for the actors, we were all being worked far
into the night. We were working at a bar location and
had been on the set for close to fourteen hours. The
second meal of the evening had been lukewarm pizza and
nerves were fraying. The director sat at the bar
between shots, staring at his script and trying to come
up with the next setup of the evening. There wasn't a
shot list or storyboard in sight. The director stared.
He mumbled. He conferred. We were all tired, hungry,
and ready to pull a mutiny. Finally, the key grip
couldn't take it anymore. He strode over to the
director and laid out the sequence for him. Loudly,
with hand gestures. The crew exchanged quiet glances.
"Good idea, let's shoot it," said the director.

Inspiration can come from any direction, in any form.
But a storyboard and/or a shot list would have shown
the crew that the director had done his homework. At
two in the morning, any leadership is appreciated.

"It is exactly what we do in cinema, combining shots that are depictive, single in meaning, neutral in content—into intellectual contexts and series."

Sergei Eisenstein
"Cinematographic Principle and the Ideogram"
Film Form, 1929

3 Text, Image and Diagram

Text, Image and Diagram:
Three Approaches to Communication

3

Many years ago I had lost my keys at a friend's house and stood in his hallway with my eyes closed, silently trying to remember where I had put them. He watched me for a while and then said with astonishment, "You're looking for the keys in your head, aren't you? You're playing back a movie of where you've been in the house and watching the images with your mind's eye."

I was puzzled. "Of course," I said. "How do you find things?" "I make a list," he replied. I was stunned. Making lists to find objects was inconceivable to me.

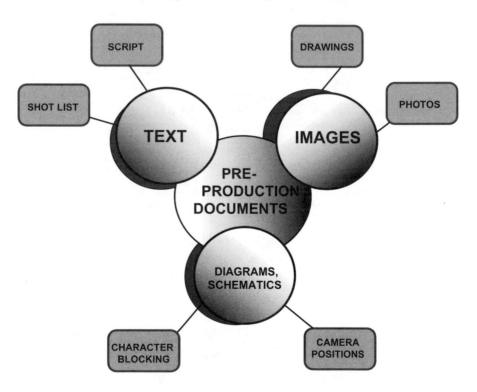

Then I had one of those "aha" moments: I realized I had made assumptions about the way other people process the world around them.

Some people understand the world primarily through words. Others through images. If we examine the differences between these two approaches, we can uncover valuable information that can be used in strategizing communication within a film crew or any other collaborative project.

The human mind is a complex, multitasking "machine" that is capable of many varieties of thought and expression. The left hemisphere is considered to control logic and language formation while the right hemisphere is credited with creative and intuitive functions. When constructing the storyboard document, we want to acknowledge this variation in thinking and include information that works on multiple levels.

TEXT	SCRIPT, SHOT LIST
DIAGRAM	OVERHEAD, SCHEMATIC PLOT PLAN, FLOOR PLAN
IMAGE	DRAWING PHOTO CGI (COMPUTER GRAPHIC IMAGERY)

Using a combination of text, images, and diagrams acknowledges that people react to these different forms of communication in varying degrees. While some of your collaborators will cull useful information from the overhead diagram, others will head straight to the images.

With this process in mind, this chapter is divided into sections detailing these three types of preproduction documents: the Shot List, the Overhead Diagram, and the Images that accompany and illustrate them.

PRODUCTION NAME: rko # 522					No. **P. 10333**
SC. # 35: INT. BAR, NIGHT				DATE SHOT	**Monday** **30 Sept:**

SLATES PRINTED	TIME FIRST SETUP GIVEN	TIME CAMERA READY	TIME FIRST TAKE	TIME SCENE COMPLETED	DESCRIPTION OF ANGLES, ACTION AND DIALOGUE
1X-3 50'	7.30	7.45	8.15	8.25 .15	Shot 1: C/U of the bar top with glasses in F.G.
2X-1 60'	8.35	8.55	8.57	8.58 .13	TRACK with bartender as he fills glasses. Med. shot with bar in mirror refection
3X-3 50'	9 (Waiting for	9.30	20.40 Bill	10.50 .27	Cut to door of bar. full shot, frontal angle. Door opens slowly letting in the light.
4X-1 30'	11 (Waiting for	11.5	11.15	11.16 .9	Med. shot of Jake scanning the crowd.
5X-2 25'	11.20	11.30	11.35	11.40	POV, PANNING the bar right and left, wide shot.
6X-6 20' T.2.Fair.	11.58 T.4.Look	12 short.T.5.	12.3 slow.	12.5 .10 Flicke Sur	Reaction shots of the bar patrons, various angles
7X-1 30' Lunch 1.	1 230 - 1.	1.15	1.20	1.25 .9	ECU of Jakes feet as he walks down the bar. TRACK back to follow.

Shot list from *Vertigo* 1958
director: Alfred Hitchcock

The Text:
Shot Lists and Terminology

The "text" in this chapter refers to the words of the shot list. The shot list is a written collection of shot descriptions, each containing information on the placement of the camera and the contents of the frame. In order to accurately convey this information, the shot list needs to use precise language that delineates the action of the scene as well as the position of the camera and its movements.

A visually specific shot list needs to include the following information:
- **Scale**
- **Angle**
- **Camera movement**
- **Blocking (of characters, vehicles, etc.)**
- **Script notations**

Scale: The relationship of the frame to the objects it presents. The frame crops the world into rectangular-shaped vistas. If the frame crops a human figure just below the shoulders, you have a close-up. If the frame allows the viewer to see an entire village, you've got a wide shot.

Angle: The relationship of the camera's position to the object(s) it is focusing on. The angle describes the position of the camera in terms of height as well as horizontal placement. If the camera is below a window and straight-on, the angle is low and frontal. If the camera is facing someone's head and is located a bit to the side, it is a three-quarter close-up, eye level.

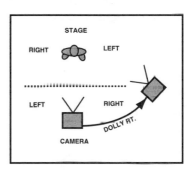

Camera movement: This term refers to the movement of the camera during a shot. It can be as subtle as a slight tilt to keep a character centered in the frame or a swooping crane shot that covers dozens of feet in a few seconds. Each camera move also has a screen direction — the right and left of the camera as seen by someone looking through the lens. The screen direction is the opposite of stage direction: If an actor were to cross to stage left (the actor's left) on a line of dialogue, then the camera would need to move screen right to follow.

Camera right and left vs. stage right and left

Character blocking: Although the shot list primarily gives information on camera placement and movement, there can also be references to the movement of what is being seen inside the frame. This includes actors' entrances and exits from the frame, movement of vehicles, or any other action that could affect the continuity of the sequence.

Script notations: In order to keep the storyboard tightly aligned with the script, small sections of dialogue or descriptions of action are sometimes added to the shot list or included in storyboard subtitles. These notations are direct quotes from the script and identify the placement of shots in relation to the action of the screenplay. For instance, a set of storyboard frames describing some over-the-shoulder shots might be accompanied by snippets of dialogue from the script marking the length of each shot.

stripes. Don't you go and get any ideas. Got it?

His father shakes his head in frustration. Then, as before, the kitchen is quiet, everyone in their own thoughts.

SHOT 16 EXT. SMALL HOUSE - DAY - FLASHBACK   #17 · C/U/34

Insert - high

A shovel is thrust into the hard thick dirt. Robbie, sweaty and dirty, digs a hole for his father. His mother steps out from the house carrying a glass of water.

#18 - bull big - format

MOTHER
Here you go, honey.

cut back - 17

Robbie takes the glass, wipes the sweat from his brow. After taking a sip he hands the glass back to his mother who stands for a moment watching Robbie resume shoveling.

insert ?

#19
Med - Cw3

MOTHER
Sometimes I wish we lived in one of those suburb neighborhoods. Course then we'd be just like everyone else. Have the same house, same car, same job. . . same paycheck.

use as master

She thinks for a second.

MOTHER
Maybe being different like we are isn't so bad. . . What do you think?

text from student project:
Damon O'Steen

Shot List Terminology

There is a saying that "a picture is worth 1000 words." But in a shot list you don't have that much space. Familiarity with the language of filmmaking is essential to creating concise descriptions of each shot.

In the pages that follow, terms that apply to the **SCALE, ANGLE, CAMERA MOVEMENT,** and **CHARACTER BLOCKING** are defined in words, diagrams, and images. This section is an illustrated glossary of film language that can be used to create a precise shot list.

SCALE

Extreme close-up (E.C.U.): A shot with a very narrow field of view that gives the impression that the camera is very close to the subject. For instance, a part of a person's face.

Close-up (C.U.): Same as above, but with a slightly larger field of view. A character's head and shoulders, for example.

Medium shot (M.S.): A shot in which the field of view is between those of the long shot and the close-up. The camera sees the actor from the waist up.

American shot (also called Hollywood, Cowboy, or Knee shot): A shot that frames a figure from the knees up.

Full Figure: Shot composed around the scale of a full human figure.

Long shot (L.S.): A shot giving a broad view of the visual field; the camera appears to be far away from the subject (the z axis).

Wide shot (W.S.): Shot composed to see a wide vista (the x axis).

Single: A shot with only one person.

Two shot: The camera frames two characters in a scene.

Insert: Often photographed by the second unit, this shot, frequently a close-up, reveals details not seen in the master shot or missed by the general coverage, i.e., a hand opening a purse and pulling out a gun.

Two-T shot: Not exactly a politically correct term; it means a shot framed from the nipples up.

ANGLE

High angle: A shot taken from an angle above the object.

Aerial shot: A very high angle shot, often accomplished with a helicopter or an airplane.

Low angle: A shot taken from the placement of the camera below the object.

High Hat shot: A very low angle shot, positioned as if it were a hat's height off the floor. The name is taken from a piece of equipment called a high hat, which is laid on the floor and is designed to hold the camera.

3/4 shot: A shot that is positioned halfway between a frontal angle and a profile. Can be either a front or a back shot.

Profile: Shot from a side angle.

Straight on, or frontal: When the camera is looking directly at an object.

Over the Shoulder shot (O.T.S.): Usually a shot of a character in conversation with a second person, whose shoulder you shoot over.

Canted frame: Also called "dutch" or "chinese" angles. The camera is tilted sideways, setting the objects off the vertical axis.

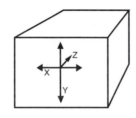

3 dimensions of movement

CAMERA MOVES

Dolly to follow

Dolly shot: Also called "tracking" or "trucking" shot. Camera travels on dolly tracks. Usually used to describe shots moving on the z axis (pushing in or pulling out).

Pan: The camera swivels on the horizontal (x) axis, often used to follow the action.

Swish Pan: A very swift pan that blurs the scene in between the starting and ending points.

Pan

Track

Tracking shot: Camera moves to left or right. Often used to follow a figure or vehicle.

Tilt: The camera pivots up and down from its base, which does not move.

Boom shot: The camera travels up and down on a boom arm. Often combines with a dolly move.

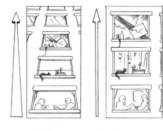

Tilt   Boom

Crane shot: A shot taken from a crane that has the ability to boom down and track in long distances without using tracks.

Car Mount: A shot taken from a camera that is mounted directly onto a vehicle.

Static shot: Any shot where the camera specifically does not move.

Car mount

Steadicam shot: A shot using the Steadicam, a camera that attaches to a harness and can be operated by a single person in handheld situations; the resulting footage will appear to be shot with the smoothness of a tracking shot.

Zoom: Refers to the movement of a zoom lens. Usually used in video.

Zoom

Zolly: A technique in which the camera dollies in and zooms out at same time, or the reverse-zoom in and dolly out simultaneously. Also called a Dolly with counter zoom. See Hitchcock (*Vertigo*), Spielberg (*Jaws*), Scorsese (*Goodfellas*).

Handheld

Smash Zoom: Very fast zoom.

Handheld: Operator braces the camera on the shoulder or at hip height. Often used in point of view shots or in documentary-style footage.

Follow shot: Any moving shot that follows an actor.

Traveling shot: Any shot that utilizes a moving camera body (a dolly is, a pan isn't).

EDITING, TRANSITIONS, AND CAMERA POINT OF VIEW

Objective shot: The camera sees the scene from an angle not seen by a character in the scene.

Subjective shot: A shot taken from the position of someone in the scene. A Point of View (P.O.V.) shot is an example of a subjective shot.

Master shot: Also called a Cover shot. Usually a medium to wide-angle shot of a scene that runs for the duration of the action.

Establishing shot: Often a wide shot of the location. It tells the audience where they are.

Coverage: All the set-ups needed to edit the scene aside from the master shot.

Set-up: Refers to the position of a camera and the lighting of a shot or shots. A "new set-up" means that the camera is moving to a new position, which also requires re-lighting.

"To envision information, and what bright and splendid visions can result, is to work at the intersection of image, word, number, art."

Edward Tufte,
Envisioning Information

Off screen (O.S.): Also called O.C., off-camera. A description of what is heard but not seen on the screen

Reaction shot: Usually a close-up of a character react-ing silently to action they have just seen or dialogue they are listening to.

Cutaway: An editing term concerning a piece of information not seen in the master or previous shot.

Reaction shot

Jump cut: Editing term for successive shots that cut in on the same axis. Also, successive cuts that disrupt the flow of time or space.

In-line Edit: Contemporary term for cutting on the same axis.

Match Cut, or Match Dissolve: Cutting or dissolving from one similar composition to another, i.e., from a close-up of a wheel to a shot of a globe of the world, so that both objects fill the same size and position in the frame.

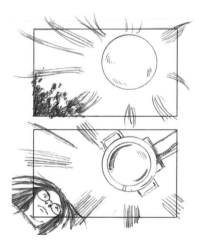

Reverse shots

Point of view shot (P.O.V.): The camera takes the point of view of a character in the scene; it sees what the character sees. Usually follows a shot of the character.

Reverse angle: A shot that is 180 degrees opposite of the preceding shot.

Exercise: Backwards Shot List
Creating a Visually Precise Shot List

When studying an art, whether it be painting, music, or filmmaking, copying the "masters" can be an illuminating and instructive exercise. As you copy a Rembrandt drawing, you are compelled to look very carefully at each decision he made regarding the composition, light, and shadow of the work. In filmmaking you can achieve a similar study by recreating a preproduction document working back from the completed film.

I call this project the "Backwards Shot List," because you take a sequence that has already been shot and edited and create a shot list, working in the opposite of the normal progression.

1. Choose a film that you want to study. It can be one that you've already seen or one that you've always wanted to get to know.

2. Play the film either on VHS, DVD, or laser disc. Try to obtain a letterboxed copy so you will see the frame as it was meant to be seen. Make sure that you can see a clear image on your screen when you pause the film.

3. Watch the entire film and make some general notes on scenes or sequences that you find compelling.

4. You will need a sequence that has between 20 to 30 shots in it. That means separate shots, not counting cut-backs to set-ups that have been previously used.

5. Play the scene you've selected, pausing the film at each cut or other transition. Write down a description of each shot, making sure that you describe the scale, angle, camera movement, and character blocking. (See examples 1 and 2, below.)

6. Number the shots, referring to cut-backs by the number that they were first assigned.

7. Shots that use a moving camera will need to be described twice: once to describe how they appear at the start and a second time for the end of the shot. In addition, describe how the camera has moved to get from the opening position to the ending one.

You will find that this exercise will sharpen your eyes as to the filmmaker's decisions regarding composition and camera angle, as well as editing. And for those of you who are new to the vocabulary of filmmaking, it will give you an opportunity to become familiar with the language.

5 Elements of Visual Shot List

1 – SCALE

2 – ANGLE

3 – CAMERA MOVE

4 – CHARACTER BLOCKING

5 – DIALOGUE OR ACTION

Ex. 1 Low angle two shot of soldier and guard. Soldier is CU in foreground, guard med. frame left.

Ex. 2 Start shot on a full, 3/4 angle of soldier as he stands and begins to cross camera right. PAN right to follow and TRACK slightly to clear attorney's back. End shot on a profile, full figure of soldier facing judges.

67

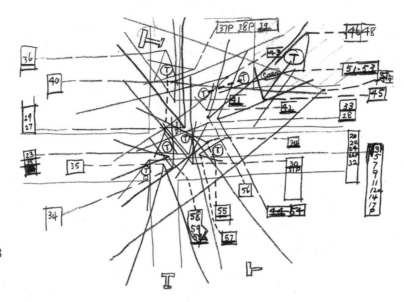

North by Northwest 1958 overhead diagram of the crop duster sequence

Overhead Diagrams

Overhead diagrams are the most powerful, universally communicative documents you can offer to your collaborators. They can sketch out the placement of the camera for different set-ups, the blocking of the actors in relation to their environment, and the position of key set pieces.

The overheads are also referred to as plot plans, floor plans, or schematics. Often the production designer or art director will sketch out each location and set design to scale. Reductions of these large drawings are perfect to use as a basis for planning out camera positions and scene blocking.

Key to understanding these documents is a familiarity with the "visual shorthand" of design. Through the use of well-placed icons, color, line width, and other eye-grabbing devices, you can lead the viewer's attention to crucial information. The following section covers some of the usual strategies for getting the point across.

Camera Position and Numbering

Each overhead diagram sets out to plot the blocking of the characters and the positions of the camera or cameras for a scene or sequence of shots. The shots are often listed in an editorial sequence and numbered accordingly. The shot list that may accompany the diagram will also be numbered, and these two documents should agree in their sequencing so that the numbers of the shot list match the numbers that mark the camera positions.

In cases where multiple cameras are being used, each camera needs its own label. You can use letters, numerals, or crew designations, anything that will get across the idea that you are assigning positions to distinctly separate camera crews.

There are times that the information needed on a particular scene or sequence is just too voluminous for a single diagram. In this case, make copies of the floor plan and plot out a portion of the information on one sheet and the rest on a second one. Layering sheets of translucent paper is another solution to the problem of tightly packed information. Using a bottom layer of white paper, start with a floor plan and then layer each scene's blocking and camera positions on subsequent layers. For reproduction, just use a single overlay and copy with the original floor plan as a back-up sheet.

Moving cameras offer another challenge. The camera has a starting point, an ending point, and a path in between. The multiple positions are still part of a single camera move, so the corresponding shot-list number will be the same. To keep things clear, subnumbering the different positions of the move is a good idea. A Steadicam shot might have four important key frames to hit on its way to its final position. Each of these should be noted on the diagram and, if an illustrated storyboard is being created, then these key positions should also be treated in corresponding frames.

Detail
Overhead diagram
Nuts 1979

Arrows

Big and little, straight and curved, with or without drop-shadows, these symbols denote direction of movement — actors walking, cars riding, or cameras rolling down the road. Arrows are one of the most powerful visual tools that you can use in overhead diagrams. They quickly attract the eye and can be used to guide the reader through the document. In addition, they can be designed to be visually distinct from each other, using dashes, line weight, or other clues to distinguish one character's blocking from another.

Color/Value

Imagine a vast plane of black and white squares and then, over to the right side, a red dot intrudes on the scene. Where does your eye go? Color can dominate the eye when used strategically. When special emphasis is needed, when you want to separate an element of information from the rest, then using color can be key.

Obviously, the color information won't reproduce well on an office copy machine, but if you are creating an overhead to be used by yourself or a small group, then adding color is a smart move, both logistically and economically.

Line Weight and Design

Thick or thin, dashes or dots, wavy or straight, even on a black-and-white document you can communicate a variety of information through simple variations of line weight and the size and shape of your lines and arrows. You can give each character a different line weight or style; you can use thick lines for camera moves and thin for character blocking. There is no industry standard for these choices. Just select a style that works for you and be consistent.

Icons

An icon is a simple representation of an object or idea. A red sign with a picture of a hand held out is an icon for the idea of "stop." In diagramming for film, video, or other media, icons can stand in for the camera, actors, or other objects about which information needs to be communicated to the crew.

The camera icon can be expressed in a number of simple forms. A small box with an angled "v" attached gives the position and a direction for the lens. Some directors do away with the box and simply draw two extended lines to show the camera's orientation. Whatever form appeals to you, use it. Just remember to keep it simple.

Tracks, pans, Steadicam shots, and other camera moves have their own icons for use in the overhead. Please refer to the diagrams on this page and the next for some additional ideas regarding these and other objects often found in an overhead.

Create a Legend

A legend is the key to a diagram's overall interpretation. If you use icons to represent your camera, characters, or their movements, a legend is a helpful guide for the reader to decipher your meaning. The legend can be placed in a corner of the diagram or along the top edge. Just don't let it interfere with the main portion of the information. Since each director, cinematographer, or designer may use his or her own icons for the camera or actors, the legend offers a quick method of identification.

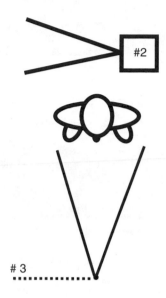

Camera and figure icons for overhead diagrams

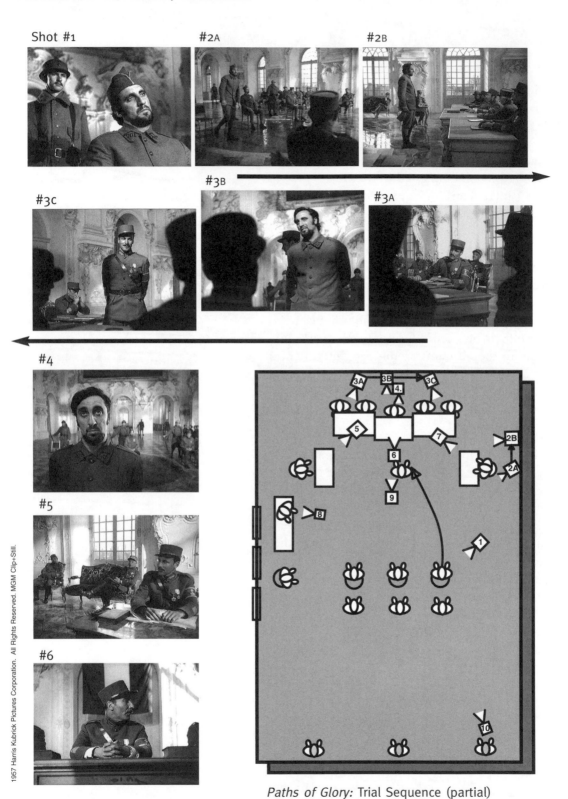

Shot #1   #2A   #2B

#3C   #3B   #3A

#4

#5

#6

Paths of Glory: Trial Sequence (partial)
Overhead diagrams of camera placement.
Compare relationships of camera icons, as
numbered, to film frames 1–10.

#7

#8

#9

#10

Exercise: Overhead Diagramming

This project will familiarize you with using icons to map out the positioning of cameras and characters in a scene from a film that has already been shot and edited.

1. Choose a film that you would like to study and know more intimately. You might consider a film directed by Orson Welles, Stanley Kubrick, Alfred Hitchcock, or Jane Campion.

2. Choose a scene from the film that has at least 10 shots. As you watch the scene again, attempt to create a proportional overhead of the environment with all the major walls, doors, furniture, streets, and buildings in place relative to each other.

3. Once this is done, watch the scene a third time, pausing the tape or the disc on each shot. Then, on the diagram, place a camera icon in the appropriate position for each of the shots. If the camera moves during the shot, be sure to indicate both the starting and the ending positions.

Exercise Example:
Paths of Glory, the Courtroom Sequence

In the following example, the overhead diagram is accompanied by still frames from *Paths of Glory* (1957), directed by Stanley Kubrick. The geography of the location is revealed in the wide shot at the end of the scene. Examine that image to get a feeling of the room and the actors' placement before exploring the rest of the shot positions in the overhead.

Paths of Glory tells the story of a regiment of French soldiers stationed on the German front in WWI. It is a study in the imbalance of power between the men who actually fight the war and those who make the decisions regarding how it will be fought. The generals are seen living in grand palaces as they decide the fate of soldiers who are dying in the trenches of the battleground.

The commanding officer orders his men to take a German position called "the ant hill." He knows that is an exceedingly difficult if not impossible task, but to further his own political ambitions he sends his men into the battle. They are mowed down before they even get to the German line and the few survivors fall back into the trenches. For failing to achieve this impossible goal, the general orders one man from each group of soldiers to be tried for treason and cowardice. If convicted, they are to be executed.

This scene is from the court martial. Kubrick moves the camera from one subjective position to another, letting us share different points of view, from the defense attorney's desk to the jury box. The overhead diagram is marked with the placement of the few set pieces in the courtroom, the blocking of the characters, and the camera positions numbered in edited shot sequence.

The Image

Storyboard images can come from various sources of inspiration. They can also be expressed in multiple ways. Whether you are an accomplished artist or someone struggling to draw a credible stick figure, there are many techniques that can help you express your vision.

Drawing

There are several highly technical methods to develop imagery these days, but most storyboard images are still created by the old-fashioned method; they're drawn using the familiar tools of paper, pencil, charcoal, and ink. These simple supplies and your mind are all that is necessary to express ideas about composition and camera position to yourself and your collaborators.

Unless you are interested in working as a professional illustrator (which requires a high level of proficiency), creating effective storyboards doesn't necessarily require great drawing skill. There are many simple approaches to drawing that can easily serve those of you who just need a tool for communication.

"Close your eyes and visualize . . ."

Alfred Hitchcock

INT. LIFEBOAT (MORNING) - TWO SHOT - KOVAC AND JOE

With all their strength they hold onto the sail rope. Back of them, in the sea, Stanley comes into the SHOT and Kovac rushes over to the side of the boat to haul him in. As he starts pulling on the rope:

Lifeboat 1943
director: Alfred Hitchcock

In the following chapters, the perspective and figure notation techniques that will be outlined will enable even a filmmaker with undeveloped drawing skills to sketch understandable, usable storyboard frames. A few days or even hours of investigation will reward you with expanded skills that will help you better communicate visual ideas.

Photograpy, Video and the Computer

I often take a 35mm camera with me when I accompany a director on location, and the zoom lens is my most important attachment. I will frequently pop off shots as I shadow the director and our collaborators around the location. Then it's off to a one-hour photo lab and I have a visual record of the angles suggested on the location scout to work from as I board up the sequences that take place on that set.

Recently I acquired a still digital camera, and that has removed some steps from the process. No buying film, loading, taking to the processing shop, and picking up. Now I simply shoot at a medium resolution (640 by 480 works well) and download straight into the photo manipulation software that came with the camera. These cameras are lightweight and can store over 100 shots on removable storage chips. They are dropping in price each month and there is a real freedom in being "film-free."

Another possibility is to use a video camera to record the angles and then print the images using a video printer or play them through a computer software program that will digitize the imagery. Digital video cameras function much like digital still cameras and can download the frames of your choice into your computer through a cable that most manufacturers supply with the camera.

Digital storyboard (detail) made with Poser and Photoshop

Many artists and filmmakers use the computer to organize as well as create original imagery. Software titles such as Adobe Premiere and Adobe After Effects allow the user to import imagery as well as design new frames and place them in an editorial sequence. In Appendix II (page 201) you will find a number of current computer applications. In addition, you may add effects and transitions between shots, such as cross-dissolves or wipes, and then play your scene back in real time. Even audio tracks can be added over the storyboard to increase the presentation's appeal.

Putting It All Together

Whether you choose to develop your imagery by high or low technical methods, keep in mind that the image must agree with the diagram, and they both must be in concert with the shot list. When all elements of the preproduction documents are in agreement, then the readers can easily move from the overhead to the image and from there to the shot list. They can in fact move in any order they care to and have each piece of information build onto the last, rather than having it cause confusion and additional questions.

Numbering System

Contemporary shooting scripts in the American film industry are broken down into individual scenes. Each time the script calls for a change in location, it will note that new location with a new scene number. Shots are numbered with a reference to the scenes that they appear in. Often the shot numbers are reset to "1" at the beginning of each scene so that you will have, for instance, Scene 5, shots 1-25, Scene 6, shots 1-26. Scene 7 shots 1-12, and so on. This method eliminates the need to renumber the storyboard if a scene happens to be cut.

Cliffhanger 1993
drawing: John Mann

The shots should be numbered so that each shot gets a separate designation. Shots that need more than one frame can be then sub-numbered with a lettering system, i.e., shot 5a, 5b, 5c, and so on. When you need to render a cutback, it is useful to just give it the same number that it used when it first appeared in the scene. This way, your storyboard will be numbered according to how many shots are planned rather than by how many cuts are envisioned in the edited sequence.

Sidebar Diagrams

There will be occasions when you plan a complex camera move and would like to include some additional information to clarify your intentions. A diagram included alongside the image can help to pinpoint your idea and eliminate the need to turn back to the overhead, which serves the entire sequence. Either in overhead or side view, this visual aid should have each position that is represented in the images marked with the image number. This way, even complicated Steadicam moves can be boarded using key frames for imagery and camera positions marked in a sidebar diagram for blocking.

Text References in the Storyboard

Along with having the shot list accompany the storyboard and overhead as a separate document, it is a good idea to transfer some or all of its information onto the storyboard itself. This usually takes the form of blocks of text that appear beneath or alongside the image. Not having the best handwriting, I take a copy of the shot list, slice it up and then paste the corresponding shot description under each image. This looks neat and makes it easy for someone to find a particular image if they're reading the shot list and want to check an image out on the storyboard.

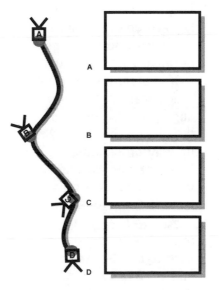

Overhead sidebar diagram of movement of Steadicam shot

"I was insecure at first (on *Boxcar Bertha*) because I had been fired from *The Honeymoon Killers* in 1968 after one week of shooting, and for a pretty good reason too. It was a 200 page script and I was shooting everything in master shots with no coverage because I was an artist! ...Of course, not every scene was shot from one angle, but too many of them were, so there was no way of avoiding a film that was four hours long. That was a great lesson. From 1968 to 1972 I was very much afraid that I would get fired again. So when I started *Boxcar Bertha* I drew every scene, about 500 pictures altogether."

Martin Scorsese,
Scorsese on Scorsese

All of this is theoretical until you try it out yourself and see what works for you. The following exercise outlines a short, simple scene, without dialogue, that you can use to practice these ideas.

Exercise: The Storyboard Moment
An Exercise for Creating a Coordinated Shot List, Overhead Diagram, and Storyboard

For the following short scene, work out an overhead diagram, a shot list, and images for a 10–14 shot sequence. Mark the camera positions and character blocking on the overhead, and be sure to use the same *aspect ratio f*or each of the frames.

1. Exterior, urban street. There is someone standing on a corner.
2. Across the street a door opens and a second person emerges.
3. The second person crosses the street to the first person.
4. They exchange something.
5. They leave, either together or apart.

Notice that the description lacks details. You need to add the story to this. Is it a western? A film noir scene? A romantic comedy? Decide on the gender of the characters, the "something" that they exchange, and feel free to embellish the story's skeletal structure.

Have fun and don't worry about the drawing, just use this exercise to become familiar with the process of working from a shot list and overhead in planning your imagery.

A student example of the Storyboard Moment follows.

OVER HEAD SHOOTING PLAN

LIGHT

RAIL ROAD

RAIL ROAD

SIGNAL LIGHT

CAR

Student example:
The Storyboard Moment
project: Roger Lee

Shot List "The Storyboard Moment"

#1   A frontal long shot of a man "A". The man "A" is walking toward the camera.

#2   A frontal Med. low angle shot of a man "B". A man who wears a nice suit is standing in front of a car.

#3   A POV of the man "B". A frontal Med. eye level shot of the man "A".

#4   A O.T.S. of the man "A". A frontal long shot of the man "B".

#5   Shot on a c/u of the man "B". As he turns his head camera PAN right a little. End shot a c/u of the man "B".

#6   A frontal Med. shot of the signal light. light changes from green to red.

#7   A frontal long low angle shot of a train. The train runs toward the camera.

#8   A O.T.S of the man "B". As the train runs across the frame, we cannot see the man "A".

#9   A frontal wide low angle shot of the train. Camera PAN left to show a man in the train who wears the hat. He drops a bottle out of the window.

#10   Open shot on a wide rear 3/4 eye level angle of the man "A". the man "A" watch the back of the train. On the right side, we can see the man "B". Camera is TRAVELING to the back side of the man "A". End shot on a O.T.S. of the man "A". A frontal full figure of the man "B".

#11   A frontal high angle of two shot of two men. the man "A"walks toward the camera.

#12   A frontal Med. angle of the man "B". As the man "A" walks into the frame from right side camera changes focus to the man "A". End shot on a profile extreme c/u of the man "A".

#13   A frontal Med. shot of the man "A". On the left side of frame, we also can see the long shot of the man "B". The man "A" put his left hand into his jacket.

#14   A frontal c/u of the man "A"'s hand which holds the bottle.

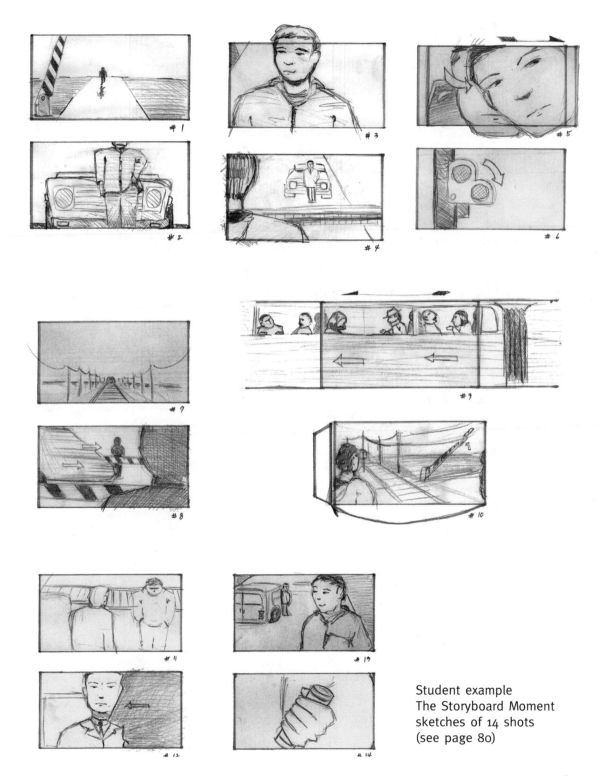

Student example
The Storyboard Moment
sketches of 14 shots
(see page 80)

Summing Up and Moving On

This chapter has explored the interworkings of Text, Diagram, and Image in the process of preproduction visualization. Each element communicates information by a different method.

• The Text: a shot list which alludes to visual aspects of the frame in words, using a specific vocabulary.

• The Diagram: an overhead view of the set with camera positions and character blocking marked down using icons and arrows. This document is both abstract and concrete in its use of simplified forms and scale drawing.

• The Image: a drawing or photo-based image that describes the composition of the frame. The most concrete of all the storyboard documents, it shows the content of the shot in static or extended frames that refer to movement of the camera.

The next chapter will discuss aspect ratios and outline the technique of extended frames for shots that use a moving camera. The technique of extending frames to show camera movement is a contemporary development in the art of storyboarding that is surprisingly easy to master and adds dynamic movement to your project.

On Fetish Finish...

During my first few months in Los Angeles I was fortunate to get a
call from the producer of the first feature on which I had been
employed. He asked me if I was available to work on some concept
sketches for a project that he was going to pitch at one of the
major studios later that month. Although I had a full-time—plus job
during the day I leapt at the chance to do some highly creative
work. The film was to take place in a variety of locations, ranging
from a Las Vegas rock-and-roll heaven to a post-apocalyptic, world-
without-music hell. There was lots of room for embellishment. I
worked nights and weekends, and when I showed the producer my ideas
in rough-sketch form he was delighted. I signed a development
contract and was slated to accompany him to the meeting at Columbia
Pictures.

Then I began to polish the rough sketches. I took all the drawings
and had them transferred to heavy illustration board. Then I spent
hours inking and coloring them in a tight, highly rendered style. I
then mounted these paintings (they were no longer sketches) and
placed them in a new, expensive portfolio I had purchased for my
trip to Hollywoodland. Wrong. When I met with the producer a day
before our scheduled meeting he took one look at the paintings (of
which I was unashamedly proud) and shook his head. "I can't take
these into the meeting," he said. "What happened to the drawings?"

I was barely breathing at this point. "I finished them" I offered.

"You killed them" he countered. "I'm pitching a treatment, not a
finished project. These paintings make it seem that we've decided
how the picture will look. I need to show them suggestions, get them
interested in the project, not present them with a finished
product."

And with a thanks and a handshake, that was the end of our alliance.
The rough sketches had been sacrificed to the icon of tight beauty,
and I'd lost out. Then again, the project didn't get funded anyway,
but that's not the point. There are times when a loose sketch is
simply more appropriate than a heavily rendered image. It's knowing
when to suggest a scene quickly rather than carve it out in stone
that will save you time and money in the end.

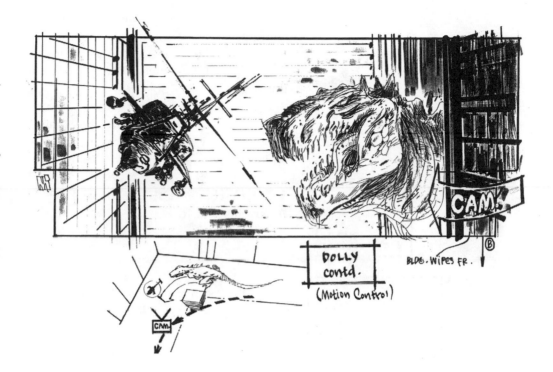

4 Aspect Ratio

"Godzilla's compositions are drawn so that they work in both 2:35 as well as 1:33. The director, Roland Emmerich, wanted to make sure that when this thing went to video it would look as good as possible. With the pan and scan technique sometimes the effects are shown off in a poor light, so he wanted to make the video look as exciting as the film. It's the first time I've ever been asked to work that way, and I think it's pretty inventive."

John Mann
Illustrator: *Godzilla* 1998

Aspect Ratio

4

Aspect ratio refers to the ratio between the horizontal and vertical dimensions of the screen. The aspect ratio of a project is determined by the medium. The width of the screen for film, television, and computers is always greater than the height.

There are several standard aspect ratios in use today. They appear in ascending order of widths below:

TV or
COMPUTER
SCREEN

1:1.33 TV, computer screen, or pre–1952 American standard

16 mm FILM or
EUROPEAN
PROJECTION

1:1.66 European standard and 16mm

AMERICAN PROJECTION

1:1.85 American standard projection ratio, post–1950s

WIDESCREEN
SUPER 35

1:2.35 70 mm, Widescreen, Cinerama, Cinemascope and other super widescreen formats

Framing History

The 35 millimeter form was developed in the early 1890s by one of Edison's assistants, W. K. L. Dickson. The format began with a 35 mm film strip 1 3/8" wide. There was an initial interest in creating a wide screen format, mostly from filmmakers who wanted to bypass Edison's patents and create their own technologies. The expense of this approach took its toll, and within a few years of its development, the 4:3 ratio had become the dominant format in the field, which remained largely unchanged for 60 years.

Before the advent of modern widescreen formats in the 1950s, there were isolated examples of filmmakers employing expanded techniques for certain sequences. Abel Gance's *Napoleon* (1927) used three synchronized cameras simultaneously in a system he called *Polyvision*. This process allowed him to create not only horizontal images with a ratio of 4:1, but also to use the elongated width to create montages of up to three images that appeared simultaneously on the screen.

As sound began to be incorporated into films, a new standard briefly appeared. The addition of a sound strip to the 35 mm filmstrip in films during the 1926-27 season caused the image to be squeezed into the remaining area. That left a slightly taller format of 1.15 to 1 for the negative image, but it also resulted in an image loss of almost 25%. To compensate for this change in shape, some projectionists began to mask out the top and bottom of the film — essentially reformatting the image to fit the theater's existing projection screen. Amid the complaints of both audiences and technicians, the Academy of Motion Picture Arts and Sciences instituted a format known as the "Academy Aperture" in an effort to create an industry standard. This 1932 document restored the format of 1.33 (or a slightly expanded 1.37) to the industry, and it remained largely unrivaled until the rising popularity of television and its co-option of the 1.33 format 20 years later.

Since the introduction of television in the mid '50s, the 1:1.85 ratio has become the standard widescreen format for projected feature projects. The wider formats are still utilized in the super 35, anamorphic, and 70 mm shooting schemes.

The Ratio and the Material
Deciding on the format in relationship to the necessities of the story

After a long reign as the ratio of choice, the "golden rectangle" began to disappear and the era of the epic widescreen frame appeared with a new, expanded horizon. The advent of such systems as Cinerama and CinemaScope in the early 1950s forever changed the experience of the audience and the canvas of the filmmaker. Instead of the slightly inflated square of 1.33 to 1, the new standard for film stretched this format into an extremely elongated rectangle of up to the 2.77 to 1 (for Cinerama), almost double the area of the original frame.

One of the first decisions regarding the visualization of a film is the choice of its aspect ratio. Widescreen creates a heightened sense of audience participation and adds an epic scope to the storytelling. Although the standard projection frame is now 1.85:1, there are specific stories that call for a different format. Recent productions that rely heavily on special effects and large action sequences have adopted the super widescreen rectangle that was so prominent in the 1950's. Summer blockbuster entertainment such as *Moulin Rouge, Jurassic Park* and *Titanic* have all been shot with the expanded ratios and make use of the added frame space to pull the audience into the spectacle of their environments.

Current independent films often focuses on stories that stress relationships and character development. These films are often shot in the prevailing 1.85:1 ratio and in addition are projected in 1.66:1 when they are shown in Europe where they have a wide audience. The 1.85 format was agreed upon as a default compromise when the size of the movie audience continued to shrink with the advent of commercial television. As widescreen became a more familiar experience, the viewing public cooled a bit to its charms and chose to take their entertainment from the more convenient box in their living rooms. In addition, the movie palaces began to give way to shopping mall multiplexes and the size of the screen shrank accordingly. Even films that were shipped with the intention of a 2.35 release format were sometimes shown in 1.85 or even 1.66 which fit the screens of the newly reduced theaters.

In keeping with the technical realities of the situation, producers reacted by shipping films that were intended to be viewed in this new standard, the widescreen as newly defined by its relationship to television. In fact, the ultimate destiny of most films is the 1:33 format of the small screen. Today movies are shot with an eye to the composition of both the original frame and the ultimate frame that will be imposed by television. A "safe action area" has been added to the viewfinders of cameras so that the cinematographers can protect their compositions for the eventual release to other media.

Computing the Aspect Ratio of the Storyboard

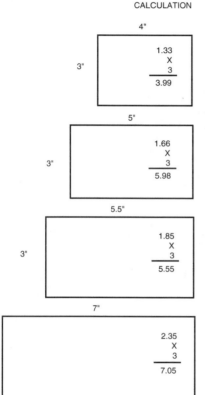

EXAMPLES OF ASPECT RATIO
CALCULATION

4"

3"

1.33
X
3
3.99

5"

3"

1.66
X
3
5.98

5.5"

3"

1.85
X
3
5.55

7"

2.35
X
3
7.05

Aspect ratio is determined by the relationship of the height of the frame to its width. The height is described by the numeral one. The width is then written as a multiple of the height. The aspect ratio of a storyboard should match the dimensions of the medium it will be released in. So if you're working in television, you need to compose your shots in a 1.33:1 drawing. A convenient size is the 3 by 4" frame, stacked vertically so that you can fit three frames on an 8 1/2" by 11" standard-size sheet of paper. For a film shooting in 16 mm, use the 1.66:1 version, which translates into a 3" by 5" frame. And for the Academy standard frame of 1.85:1, the size will work out to 3" by 5 1/2." These are just suggestions, as some directors prefer to work with only one image per page, while others choose to work from thumbnail sketches that might number up to 15 on a standard-size size sheet.

To calculate a correctly proportioned frame, start with the size of paper you'll be working with. You can orient the sheet either vertically or horizontally, but take into account that the script is a vertical document, and you might want to place the boards inside it or copy them on the reverse side of the script pages. Next, decide on how many frames you would like on one sheet of paper. Once you've settled on a height for the frame, let's say 4", multiply it by the aspect ratio of your media.

For example, if you're working on a picture shot in Cinemascope, then the width of the frame will be 2.35 times the height. Multiply 4 X 2.35 and you arrive at the width of the frame, which will be approximately 9.4". This method will give you the general storyboard dimension for your project.

TV Formatting: Changes to the Original Frame

Letterboxing

In recent years, with the popularity of cable stations that are aimed toward an audience of film purists, the practice of letterboxing films for television is becoming more common. The letterbox presents the film in its original format, with a black border filling the unused space at the top and bottom of the TV frame. This allows the entire width of a 1.85 or a Cinemascope film to be shown, while the height of the frame is reduced to only a portion of the television screen. Many DVD titles specialize in releasing letterbox versions of new and classic films, a format popularized earlier by the laser disc. Please refer to the Appendix I (page 193) for a list of DVDs which include storyboards.

Pan-and-Scan

This is an alternative to the method of letterboxing and refers to a reformatting of the original composition. The pan-and-scan technology selects sections of imagery from the projection version and plugs them into the target aspect ratio, usually the 1.33:1 of television. This technique seeks to follow the action around the frame and will often result in cutting out secondary pieces of visual information that were crucial to the balance and meaning of the original composition. At its worst, the pan-and-scan method leaves little more than half of the frame and is a shadow of the filmmaker's original vision.

Summary

It is imperative that when you work on pre-production visualization, you create frames that accurately reflect the intended aspect ratio of your project. Whether you are working in video or Cinemascope, the format offers you specific challenges in composition and framing. If you have the luxury of choosing among formats, then viewing films or videos using letterboxed examples can help you to decide which one will best serve your project. These films can also be excellent sources for ideas on composition and camera movement.

Framing Samples

The next three pages offer generic framing examples that may be photocopied and used for a variety of projects.

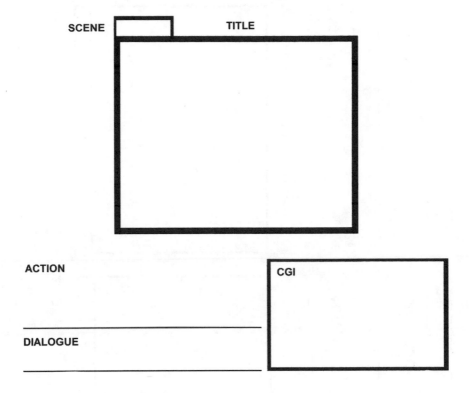

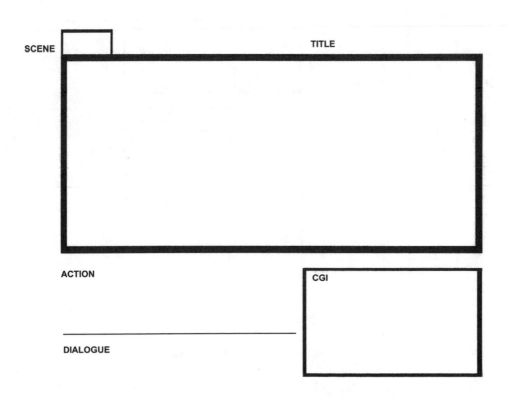

SCENE _____

SHOT # _____

ACTION

DIALOGUE

FX

SHOT # _____

ACTION

DIALOGUE

FX

PAGE _____

SHOT # _____

ACTION

DIALOGUE

FX

PAGE ____

SHOT #

ACTION

DIALOGUE

FX

SHOT #

ACTION

DIALOGUE

FX

SHOT #

ACTION

DIALOGUE

FX

Frame Viewers

There are a number of viewfinders on the market that, without a camera, will allow you to view a scene in the appropriate aspect ratio and a variety of lens lengths. They are commonly seen around the neck of directors and cinematographers and have the appearance of a lens on a cord.

These devices often cost hundreds of dollars; while they are an excellent investment for the working professional, an alternate aid to framing up your shots can be easily and inexpensively produced using the following guides. Feel free to photocopy or cut them out of the book and make up these lightweight tools in a variety of ratios. You will find that by looking through the opening of the viewfinder, extending your arms and then pulling them slowly in, you can approximate a number of lens lengths.

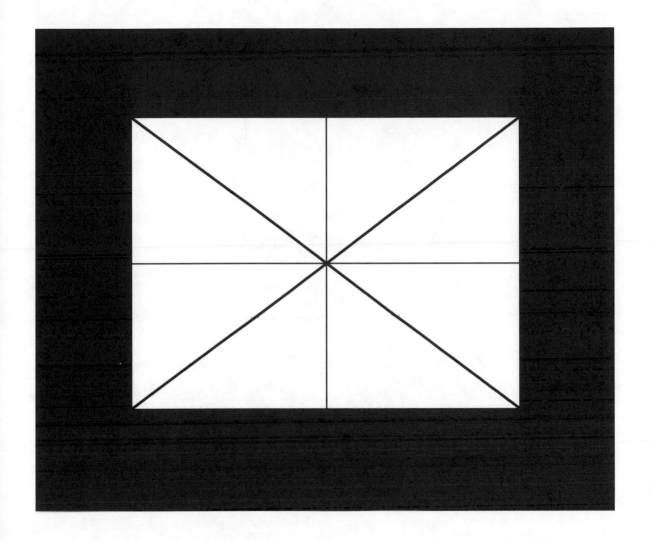

FRAME VIEWER: 1.33 ASPECT RATIO

TELEVISION AND COMPUTER MONITOR

TO USE:

* CUT OUT ON DOTTED LINES (SEE REVERSE OF SHEET)
* AFFIX TO BOARD OR FOAMCORE BASE
* TRIM BOARD TO FRAME SIZE, CUT OUT INNER BOX

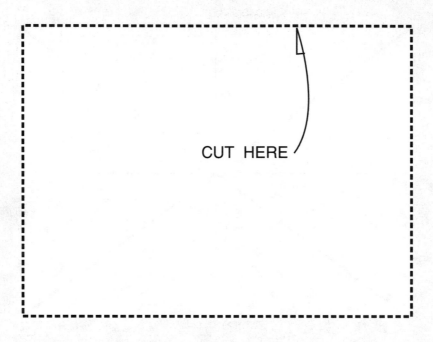

CUT HERE

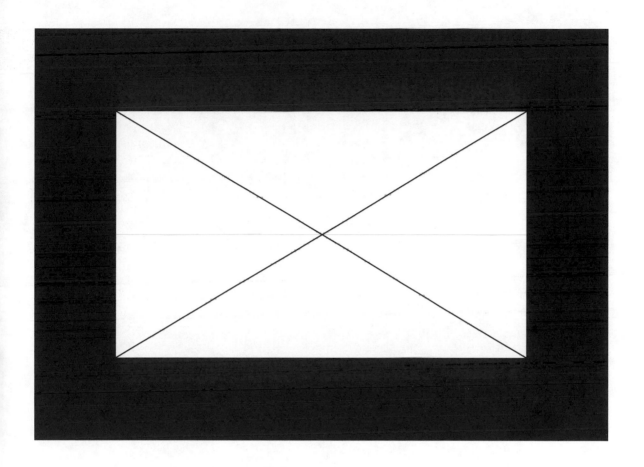

FRAME VIEWER: 1.66 ASPECT RATIO

16 MM FILM AND EUROPEAN PROJECTION

TO USE:

* CUT OUT ON DOTTED LINES (SEE REVERSE OF SHEET)
* AFFIX TO BOARD OR FOAMCORE BASE
* TRIM BOARD TO FRAME SIZE, CUT OUT INNER BOX

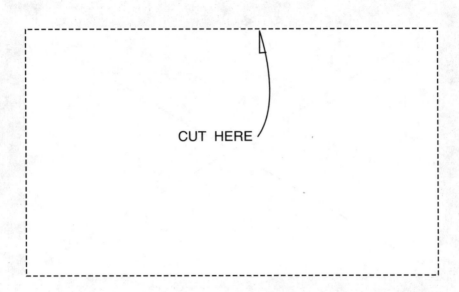

CUT HERE

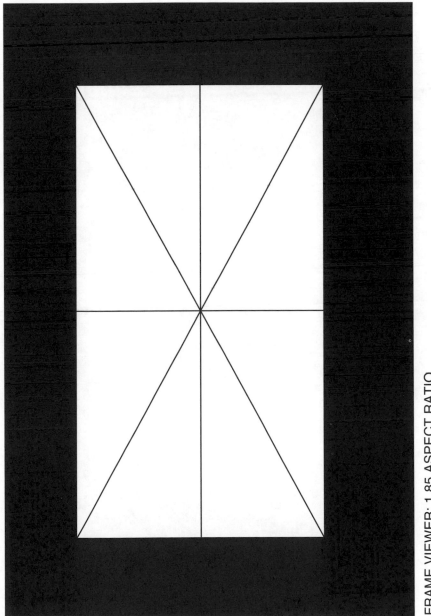

FRAME VIEWER: 1.85 ASPECT RATIO

AMERICAN PROJECTION (ACADEMY STANDARD)

TO USE:

* CUT OUT ON DOTTED LINES (SEE REVERSE OF SHEET)
* AFFIX TO BOARD OR FOAMCORE BASE
* TRIM BOARD TO FRAME SIZE, CUT OUT INNER BOX

City of Westminster College
Paddington Learning Centre
25 Paddington Green
London W2 1NB

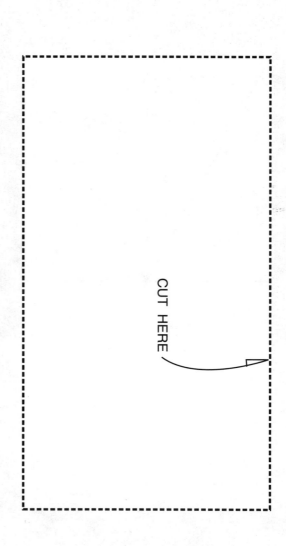

CUT HERE

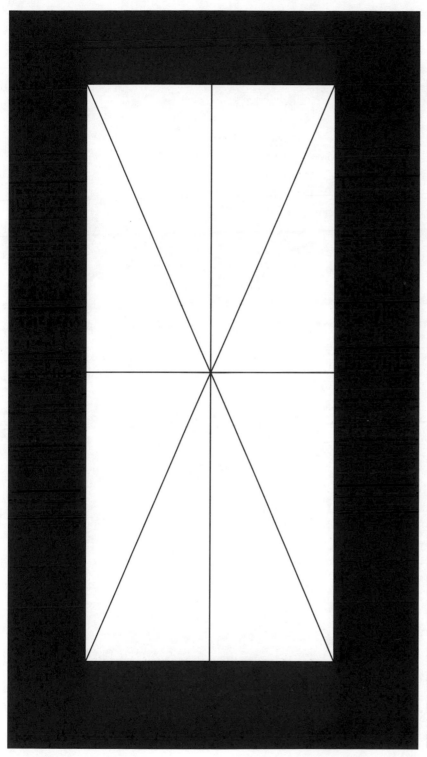

FRAME VIEWER: 2.35 ASPECT RATIO

WIDESCREEN. SUPER 35, SCOPE

TO USE:

* CUT OUT ON DOTTED LINES (SEE REVERSE OF SHEET)
* AFFIX TO BOARD OR FOAMCORE BASE
* TRIM BOARD TO FRAME SIZE, CUT OUT INNER BOX

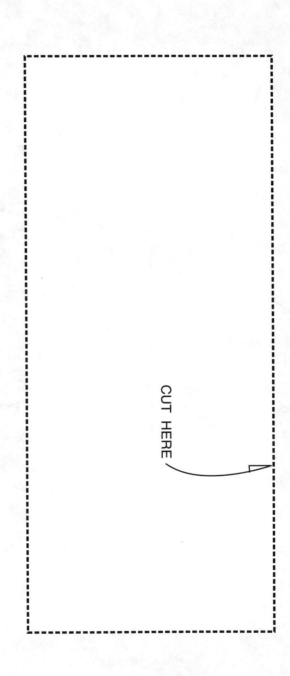

CUT HERE

Set Harassment

I was standing off camera watching a scene being shot. The director
called "cut" and as the leading man walked past, he grabbed me and
proceeded to give me a very wet and unwanted kiss on the lips.

I was shocked. I had spoken to this man a couple of times, but his
advance was completely unexpected and not in the least romantic. This was
only my second film and I was an assistant to the production designer. In
other circumstances I might have let my outrage show, but in that
situation my career seemed on the line. So, what do you do? Keep your
mouth literally and figuratively shut? Or raise a stink and demand an
apology from the actor and/or the producing organization? Tough call.

The gender split on the set seems to run about 1 to 10 in favor of the
guys. Great odds if you're a woman looking to hook-up with someone, but a
difficult split if you are interested in some workplace peace and
privacy. For anyone considering an on-set career, the handling of on-set
advances can be an issue to consider.

Humor can be a great ally. You will be working in tight quarters and for
long hours with the rest of the cast and crew. Having a few good brush-
off lines that show you can be a good sport while placing limits on your
availability will come in handy. If the gentleman persists in unwanted
or crude remarks, than a private chat, out of earshot of the rest of the
crew, might do the trick. The get-the-girl atmosphere that is sometimes
fostered on sets can carry a sense of sport about it and no one wants to
be rebuffed in front of colleagues.

A straight, serious request for professional behavior presented with a
no-hard-feelings attitude will often lighten the mood. It can calm down
a situation which can be detrimental to both getting the job done and
enjoying it in the first place.

I kept my mouth shut about the actor's errant tongue and was plagued with
invitations to his trailer and calls at home. It was clear to me that he
was after a quick, uncomplicated encounter and was using his position to
force the point. I am not proud of my handling of this situation. I kept
my mouth shut, just smiled at him, and tried to steer clear of his path.
After the show wrapped I finally got around to telling him to leave me
alone.

The imbalance of power in these types of situations can be unnerving.
In a freelance business, one nasty outburst can haunt you for years. It
takes practice, but standing up for your personal rights with a sense of
humor and forgiveness can have a long-lasting effect on your relationship
to the job and your co-workers.

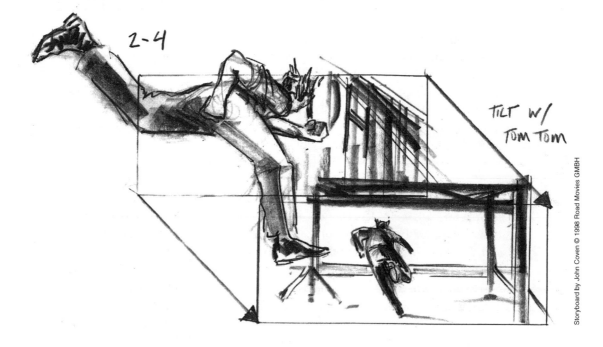

2-4

TILT w/ TOM TOM

5 Extended Frames

"I'll often use extended frames for tracking shops, panning shots, and tilting shots. Sometimes I use the entire vertical length of the page for a craning shot. You need to be able to communicate the entire shot in that one image. The dimension that you have in film that you don't have in illustration is time. The art of storyboarding is in choosing the right moment of time for illustration. You need to be able to communicate the entire shot in that one image."

John Coven
illustrator: *The Usual Suspects*, *X-Men*

Introduction to Extended Frames

5

This chapter aims to familiarize you with the idea of extended frames. The extended frame format allows the storyboard artist to reference the time and space elements of filmmaking. The frame of film or television media is defined by its aspect ratio. This shape contains the visual information for a single, static shot. The single image held in this frame can only express one moment, a fraction of the time that the shot will actually last. One question that often comes up in the study of storyboarding is which moment to represent when you only have this single reference to the proposed shot.

To find the answer, it is useful to imagine how the shot begins and how it ends, and ask yourself: *What are the important visual changes that occur between these two points?* Perhaps someone enters the frame, or an argument breaks out and the shot covers some of the action. In these two circumstances you would want to focus on the large movements in the shot. For example, the moment a new character enters the frame, represent the movement with an arrow coming from outside the frame. On the other hand, visualizing a moment in the heat of the argument would give you an opportunity to create a composition that takes advantage of the emotion and action of the scene.

If you are an accomplished illustrator, then using forced perspective in a shot that includes active blocking can help to give the viewer a sense of the excitement and deep cinematic space. If your drawing skills are more modest, then go for a general sense of the scene's blocking. A well-placed arrow can tell your collaborators what you have in mind even if the details are broad and general. Again, focus on visualizing the starting and ending points of the shot, and then determine if you can express what you need the shot to do in one frame.

If you need more than one image to accomplish this, then one option is to create images that express two or more key frames of the shot.

The chapter will cover the following camera movements:

- Static
- Pan, Track, Swish Pan (horizontal shots)
- Dolly (in/out), Zoom (in/out)
- Tilt, Boom, Vertical Pan (vertical shots)
- Crane
- Zolly (zoom with counter dolly)
- Specialty moves, such as the handheld shot and the Steadicam

The Frame as an Icon of Movement

Imagine a storyboard frame as a moving entity. The frame represents the picture plane of the camera. When you want to communicate the imagery seen by the camera's moving viewpoint, you can utilize one of two methods. You can draw, in separate frames, what the shot will look like at the start of the move and what it will look like after the move is over. This will give you two static representations of what the audience will see.

The second choice is to extend the edges of the frame to encompass the scope of the entire shot. If the camera is to travel the length of a room, for example, and the visual content of the shot changes completely from the start to the finish, then the aspect ratio of the shot can be doubled on the horizontal axis. If the camera rotates in a 270-degree arc, the triple width might be needed to show the entire breadth of information. You only need to extend the frame to include the visual information within the camera move. Sometimes this will be only a small amount, as in a shot that adjusts to the movement of a character with a subtle tilt and panning motion. In this case you might just use two slightly overlapping frames to get your point across.

Both methods are acceptable. You might opt for the second version and use extended frames when the sequence you are planning has many camera moves. The pages will be more dynamic in design and show the camera's movement more fluidly. The static method, using individual frames of the same size and shape, can be used when you need to save time and print out sheets of frames in advance.

The Cotton Club 1984
illustrator: Harold Michelson

I often use my computer to print the storyboard frames. I have stored files with frames of different aspect ratios and various extended frame shapes. When I have a shot list ready, I print out the number of static frames needed, the extended frames that are already stored, and then create any new frame shapes that are necessary. Next to each frame I have a text box printed to hold the shot list information.

In addition, it is useful to design a place on the sheet for the shot and scene numbers. It is easier to read the board if you are consistent with the placement of each item of information. If you place the scene number on the top right of the first sheet, continue the practice for every scene that you board. The shot numbers should be close to the frames, and in most cases the numbering system for each scene will start from "1." This way, if a scene is omitted, the missing section will not throw off the numbering sequence.

In the pages that follow, you will find various examples of frame extensions and explanations of the camera movements that motivate them. As you examine each frame, understand that the camera movement being illustrated is only one example of that particular move. If the camera is booming and tracking, then the combination of frames that stack vertically as well as horizontally will be needed, but there are many different combinations that can be formed using this basic concept.

At the end of this section an exercise called "The Single Image Storyboard" will lead you through a storyboard sequence created with a single photo image. This will allow you to practice the technique of creating extended frames without being concerned about drawing interior imagery. This technique can only be mastered by hands-on use, so begin to experiment with it on your next sequence of shots. Your board will be a more dynamic expression of the film or video that is yet to come.

Static Frame and Additional Information for the Storyboard Page

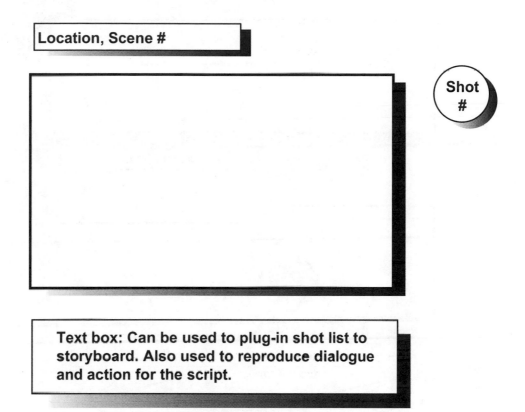

Location, Scene #

Shot #

Text box: Can be used to plug-in shot list to storyboard. Also used to reproduce dialogue and action for the script.

Horizontal Movement

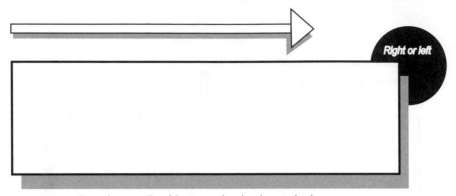

Panning or Tracking on the horizontal plane

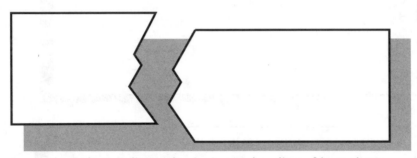

Broken plane indicates beginning and ending of long shot

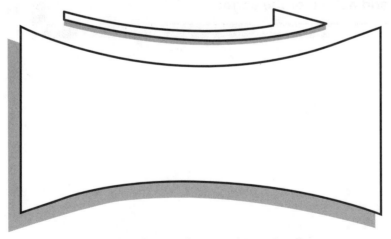

Panning frame often used in animation

Vertical Movements
Boom or Vertical Pan (Tilt)

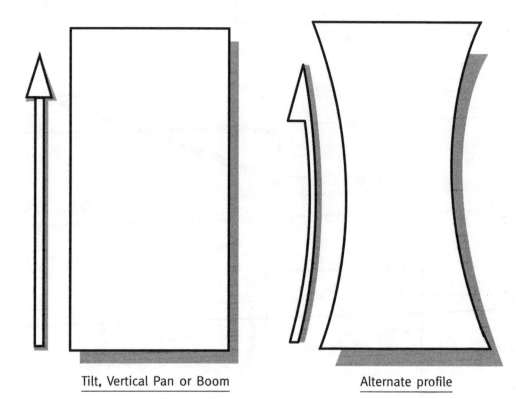

Tilt, Vertical Pan or Boom   Alternate profile

Movement on the Vertical and Horizontal Axes

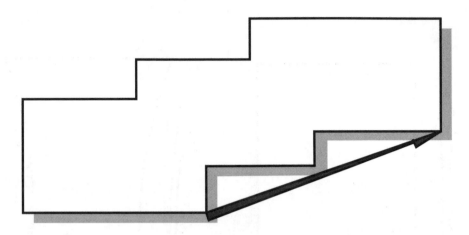

Pan or Track with a Tilt or Dolly (Vertical and horizontal movement at the same time)

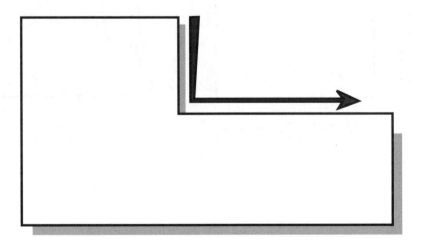

Tilt/Boom down and then Pan/Track screen left

Combination of Movement
In/Out and Up/Down

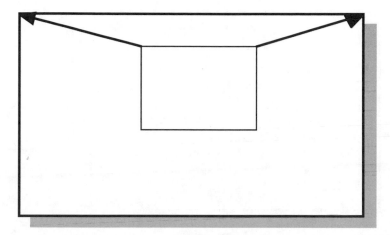

Dolly back or Zoom out (Dolly or Zoom in by changing direction of arrows)

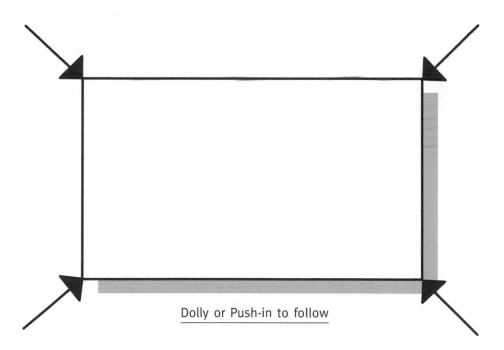

Dolly or Push-in to follow

Three-Way Movement
Over, Up or Down and In or Out

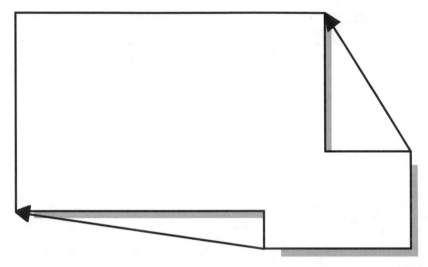

Dollying or Zooming out, Panning or Tracking to the left and Booming or Tilting up

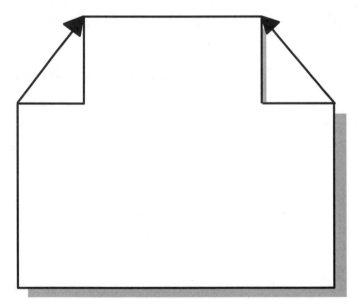

Dolly/Zoom in and Tilt or Boom up. Can reverse arrows for moves out.

Movement into the Depth of the Frame

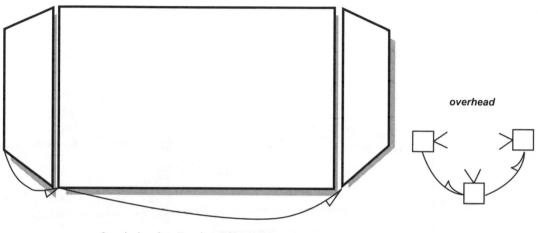

overhead

Semi-circular Track with Counter-pan

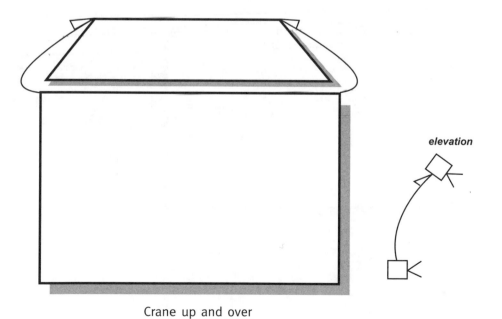

elevation

Crane up and over

Cranes and Circular Tracking Shots

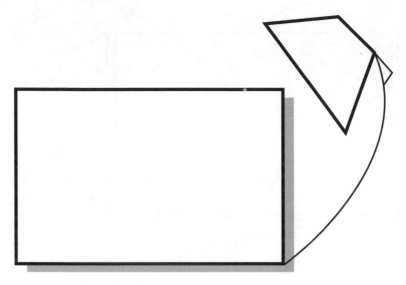

Crane up and to the right, Tilt down to keep action centered

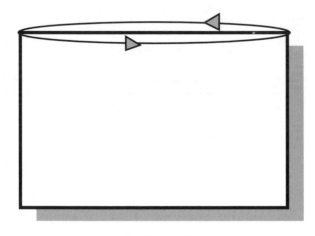

360 degree Pan

Specialty Moves

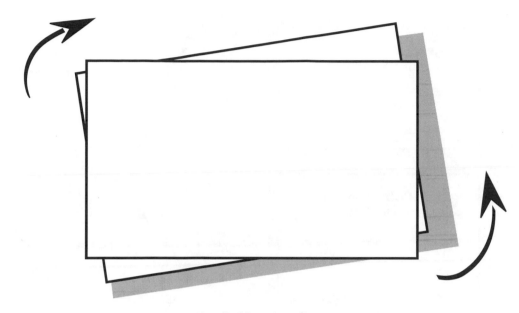

Handheld or Steadicam

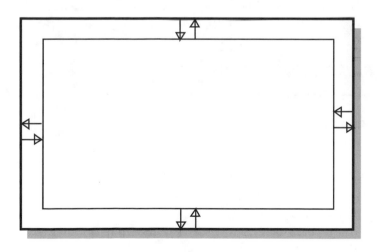

Zolly, aka Dolly with a Counter Zoom

Steadicam and
Lengthy Hand-Held Movement

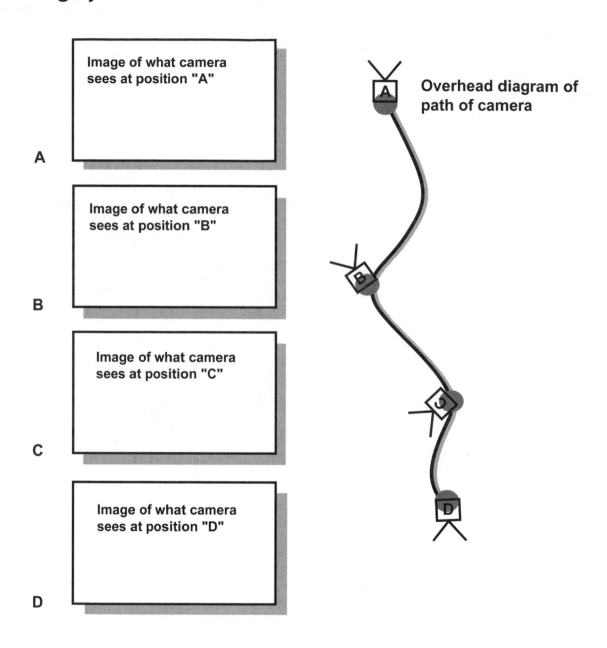

Image of what camera sees at position "A"

A

Image of what camera sees at position "B"

B

Image of what camera sees at position "C"

C

Image of what camera sees at position "D"

D

Overhead diagram of path of camera

Exercise: The Single Image Storyboard

The following exercise offers an opportunity to practice using extended frames. It also can give you a good workout in editing.

1. Choose an image. It can be a photo, painting, or tapestry, just as long as it has good narrative content. The best images have a good mix of foreground, mid-ground, and background elements.

2. Create multiples of the image, either on a copying machine or in a computer application that allows image manipulation, such as Adobe Photoshop.

3. Using a consistent aspect ratio, crop out various shots from the whole. Try to find 8-14 shots, and have at least four that use a moving camera.

4. Arrange the "shots" onto paper and experiment with various arrangements.

5. Paste in place and add arrows where needed. Don't add text, this is a "silent" film.

6. Show the sequence to a group and ask someone to talk their way through the narrative.

For an extra challenge, try to make the sequence tell a different story than the original image.

"The Japanese approach drawing from quite a different direction than our method. They take an image of the branch of a cherry tree. The pupil cuts out from this whole, with a square, and a circle, and a rectangle: compositional units. He frames a shot!"

Sergei Eisenstein
"Cinematographic Principle and the Ideogram"
Film Form, 1929

Single Image Storyboard:
An Example, "Tijuana Rally"

1.

2.

← Pan left

3.

4.

Static

Static

5.

Dolly out

6.

Static

7.

Boom up

8.

Tilt down/ Pan left

9.

Dolly right

10.

Static

123

I Want it Cheap, Fast and Ugly

I was called in for an interview to storyboard an episode of an
hour-long dramatic series for ABC. This was a fairly unusual
request, because most episodic dramas have very short preproduction
schedules. For that reason, as well as financial concerns, most of
these series forego the storyboarding process.

This particular show had some unique challenges. They explained to
me that most of the episode was to take place on a bridge at night.
And a portion of the story took place on top of that bridge. The
production manager had estimated that they would need five days to
shoot the bridge sequences. The problem was, they were only able to
secure the location, a bridge in downtown Los Angeles, for a single
night.

The production designer planned to build a full-size model of the
lower portion of the bridge in a parking lot at the studio. Then, on
one of the stages, the top of one of the bridge's arches would be
constructed. They needed to storyboard to plan out which shots had
to be accomplished at the original location, which could be taken on
the parking lot set, and finally, what needed to be done on the
stage set.

The producer and director took a look at my portfolio and asked when
I could start the project, as shooting was scheduled for the next
week. I agreed to start immediately, and then the producer asked if
he could speak with me privately for a moment. (Watch out for this
one, my mother's voice whispered in my head.) When we were alone in
his office, the producer closed the door. He walked over to me and
said in a soft, intense voice, "I want them fast, I want them cheap,
and I don't care if they're pretty."

He wanted the job done and me out of there as soon as possible. Only
in the most dire of circumstances would this producer agree to hire
an illustrator. And he didn't want the clock ticking his dimes away
for any longer than was absolutely necessary. I called my assistant
and we hammered out close to 150 frames in the next 3 days. I
delivered the project by the weekend and they were pretty in spite
of it all. No extra charge.

Lifeboat 1944

6 Composition

"I never look through the camera, you know. When in doubt I draw a rectangle then draw the shot out for [the cameraman]. The point is that you are, first of all, in a two-dimensional medium. Mustn't forget that. You have a rectangle to fill. Fill it. Compose it."

Alfred Hitchcock

Composition

Introduction

6

There are two ways of viewing a film: passively and actively. The passive viewer sits back and enjoys the show, rarely asking why particular choices of composition or camera placement have been made. The active viewer not only sees and hears the film, but also is involved in exploring it on a deeper level — one which is not immediately apparent to the casual viewer.

Elements such as the color of the setting, the movement of the camera, and the position of objects or placement of people within the frame are experienced on a subconscious level. Sometimes this information is recognizable on the first viewing (especially if you are an active viewer and pay attention to these details), but it often requires a second or third viewing to see past the action and dialogue in a film and pick up the subtleties of its visual storytelling.

By taking an active role you can begin to participate in the thought processes and active decisions that are used to form the work of art. Once you have learned how to actively observe, you will find that in addition to enjoying the film as entertainment you will be investigating each image as an expression of the narrative. The graphic, two-dimensional structure of the frame is a powerful medium of communication. A great deal can be absorbed by looking at the various ways that directors, cinematographers, and art directors can manipulate the composition of the frame to maximize its use as a strong storytelling device.

This chapter will cover different approaches to breaking down the frame and its composition into their component design parts and investigating how decisions of line, form, depth, and texture affect the "read" of the picture.

The first section will explore the relationship between composition and story. The narrative structure of a film and the atmosphere and tone of its story can be read in its images as well as the dialogue and action. Visual choices affect the way the audience understands the characters and their surroundings. Different approaches to composing the frame such as the use of open versus closed framing and other practices will be explored, along with ideas on positive and negative space and other fundamentals of composition.

The rest of the chapter will focus on the formal aspects of design as it applies to the film and video frame — including graphic composition as expressed in strategies of symmetry, balance, and randomness, among many other forms. The qualities of value, contrast, and texture will be covered as well.

One note of caution: There can be a tendency toward trying to create a design template for the purpose of expressing story and character through imagery. Beware! Looking for absolute meanings to attach to specific camera angles or colors can be misleading. Each shot must be considered in the light of what has come before it and what is to come after it. It is the context that imparts meaning, not a slavish adherence to formulas.

Composition: Formal Considerations in the Design of the Frame

Overview of Chapter:

The Frame
- Positive and Negative Space
- Depth cues
- Overlap, focus, scale
- Symmetry
- Balance
- Series
- Randomness
- Shape
- Circle, arc, square, triangle, spiral, rectangle, linear
- Diagonal, horizontal, vertical
- Texture
- Contrast, value
- Framing devices
- Open and closed framing

October 1927
Example of randomness

The Frame

Our world has an endless horizon. Look up, down, turn in any direction and you are met with a seamless cyclorama of imagery. The frame is a tool that we use to break up this panorama into digestible pieces. The frame is a cropping device that snips away what we, as designers and directors, do not want the audience to see. The audience can be placed in a unique relationship with a character or environment through the specificity of these choices. The possibilities are limitless.

The manipulation of point of view is a powerful aspect of storytelling that is played out in the placement of objects and/or people inside the frame. The frame is a mobile window that can open onto any section of a scene, at any distance we desire. Because of this mobility, we can present the world with a more precisely composed structure than we usually encounter in our everyday lives. The camera can structure images of the world that are remarkable in their symmetry or randomness, their balance or internal geometry. Before exploring the specifics of these compositional strategies, there are a few general topics of two-dimensional design that need to be introduced.

Positive and Negative Space

There is a well-known illusion in which, while a person gazes at a drawing of a candlestick, it seems to transform into a double portrait. Using a contour that can be read in two ways to separate the black and white areas of the frame creates the illusion. The eye reads the white area as an object and sees the image as a candlestick, or favors the dark areas and sees them as silhouetted profiles.

This perceptual trick illustrates the play of positive and negative space. Positive space in a composition is an area that defines an object or figure. It is form. Negative space is that area which defines the space around these forms. Both spaces require a designing eye, but often the negative space is ignored, considered to be somehow less important than the positive space in frame composition.

In fact, they are locked together in a dance of mutual support. A shot of an apple sitting on a table is as much about the atmosphere around the apple as the apple itself. And aside from aesthetic considerations, the negative space can also hold the possibility of movement, surprise, or danger coming from outside the frame. The examples of film frames in this chapter highlight the various approaches to composition.

October
Example of positive and negative space

DEPTH IN THE FRAME

Depth within the frame is illusory. The frame or screen is a flat form; the depth we perceive is a result of fooling the eye — we believe that we see a third dimension where there is none. There are a number of visual cues that the eye and mind recognize as references to depth:

- A change in scale
- Overlapping objects
- Changes in focus or depth of field
- Color shifts

These visual cues imply the existence of a space beyond the screen. Learning to recognize and use them offers expanded control over the visual construction of each shot.

Change in Scale

A friend of mine was working as a set dresser on a feature being produced in Los Angeles. One day during preproduction, the set decorator gave him a list of items to round up for the next set. My friend noticed a large array of children's items on the list, from clothes to outdoor furniture to tiny lighting fixtures. He was confused. There were no children in the script. Could the designer be padding the shopping list with objects he needed for his own home?

The answer came the next day when they arrived at the set, which was built on a sound-stage. Most of the story they were filming took

3/4 size buildings   **full size building**

Queens Logic 1988
production designer: Edward Pisoni

place in a New York apartment and its rear courtyard. In order to make the most of the limited stage space, the production designer designed the "buildings" surrounding the "yard" to 1/2 and 1/4 scale. The little clothes and furniture were to grace the balconies and windows of the scaled-down buildings, which through the camera appeared to be in perfect proportion and a great distance away.

Raise your hand up so that it is positioned about 12 inches from your face. Now look beyond your hand to some architectural element in the room or on the street outside a window. Notice the relative size of your hand to the wall or the door. There is a severe diminishing of perceived size as an object recedes into the distance.

Art directors can use this knowledge to fool the eye into thinking that a set is much larger than it truly is. If you build a wall in the distance at half scale, the audience will "read" the wall as being much farther away. Increase the scale and the eye will tell the brain that the wall is much closer. Place a tall actor in the middle ground of a composition and a shorter actor's head in the foreground will be even with his.

Alexander Nevsky 1938

Overlapping Objects

M 1931

An infant thinks that when her mother disappears into the next room she no longer is part of the world. Through repeated experience the child learns that out-of-sight does not mean out-of-existence. We grow and begin to know the world in more explicit ways, and the sight of a body partially hidden by a piece of furniture does not panic us into calling 911 for fear that the body has somehow lost its legs. We learn early on that appearances are deceiving, and the image of one object obscuring another is interpreted as a spatial cue.

In film, overlapping objects occur when the camera is positioned so that one form partially obscures another. When you raise or lower the camera, more of the hidden object will come into view. Our eyes judge distance and depth by the density of the superimposed items and the amount of visual information that is hidden.

Change in Focus and Depth of Field

Focus and depth of field are a function of the lens length and the aperture used during exposure of the film. A shot with a narrow field of focus can emphasize a figure, for example, by throwing the surrounding environment into an indistinct haze. This forces the audience to concentrate on one plane of space while de-emphasizing the remaining depth of the frame. Using a wide-angle lens will offer a much deeper depth of focal plane and integrate the object into its environs. A change in focus during a shot, a rack focus, leads the audience's eye through the frame by changing the plane of focus as they watch.

Another, though less common, use of depth of field can be found in the zolly, or zoom-with-a-counter-dolly shot. In this camera move, the characters or object being viewed will often stay the same relative scale while the lens length changes. The scale is maintained by the movement of the camera on a dolly that counters the zooming activity of the lens. The composition does change though, as seen in the following examples.

Close-up with wide lens before Zolly

Close-up with long lens after Zolly

COMPOSITIONAL STRATEGIES

Film and video are media that primarily use representative imagery to tell their stories. But we can also look to abstract design principles for ways to move the eye around the frame. Each frame or shot can be composed according to one or more two-dimensional design strategies. Even so-called "random" or "documentary-style" setups can be devised using these compositional structures.

Symmetry

A symmetrical frame is one that is always balanced: For every form and line on one side of the frame, there is a corresponding form or line on the opposite side. Symmetry is also characterized by an "angle of reflection." This angle is an imaginary line that runs through the frame and separates the two mirror-image halves vertically, horizontally, or diagonally.

Angle of reflection

There is also a type of symmetry that is known as "radial symmetry," where rather than a line of reflection, the symmetry is constructed around a center point. Forms that radiate out from a pivotal spot create balance.

A one-point perspective setup often creates a symmetrical frame automatically. When the camera's picture plane is parallel to the set and the camera is positioned in a central place relative to a wall or a street, the resulting frame will often have a strong symmetrical element.

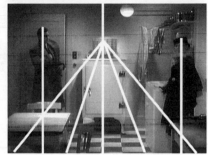

The symmetry of one-point perspective

Asymmetry

The asymmetrical frame is more than a frame that simply lacks absolute symmetry. It has, as an overriding aspect of its design, a variety of forms placed without regard to any mirroring plan.

Balance

In the three-dimensional world, balance is a matter of physical weight. Circus performers, construction workers, and grocers all depend on the accurate measurement of weight in order to perform their tasks with ease and precision. In the 2-D world of the screen, issues of balance are measured differently. Size, scale, value, and color, among other elements, create visual weight.

M

Potemkin

The balanced frame is equally weighted on both sides of the composition. Balance is not mutually exclusive to an asymmetrical frame. A distribution of differently scaled objects, contrasts in value, or even variations in color can create an asymmetrical composition. The element of balance is something that can be sensed, if not measured. It creates a world in which the eye travels unimpeded around and through the various forms it encounters.

Imbalance

October

Imagine a frame composed of a feather on one side and an elephant on the other. What does your eye travel to first, and where does it return? The imbalanced frame has a weight problem. This is not to say that there is something necessarily wrong with an imbalanced frame. The weight issue can always be worked to the advantage of the director or designer. If you are aware of the situation, you can utilize the composition to manipulate your audience's attention to a particular object or event. It is also an effective way to allude to the space outside the frame.

Series

Imagine a camera facing the side of a large office building. Rows of windows, all the same shape and size, fill the frame. The only variety comes from small, individual touches that are visible in each cubicle. This is a frame that is structured by a series.

October

A series is created by a repetition of form or line within the frame. The eye is met with a pattern that is repeated over and over. The viewer's attention will be immediately drawn to any element that is out of step in the established order.

Randomness

Randomness is more than an absence of order. It is an arrangement that alludes to a world that has not been touched by the manipulation of human hand or mind. This approach is deceptively difficult to achieve. In fact, it may take a great deal of planning to create a composition that looks random. Our minds demand order. Even when we attempt to create a less–than–orderly arrangement of objects, going against the mind's natural inclination to order is surprisingly difficult, and the "ordering" human hand can often still be seen or sensed in the design. Only skillful blocking that carefully mirrors chaotic movement will create a crowd scene that appears disorderly.

October

Alexander Nevsky

Stagecoach 1939

Lines and Shapes

A line is a vector, a connection of one point to another; it plots direction. Within the frame it can act as a powerful guide to lead the eye from one place of interest to the next. There are many examples of compositions that use linear strategies to structure the frame. Horizontal, vertical, and diagonal lines are among the most commonly used in film, video, and other two-dimensional projects.

Film and video share a compositional similarity in that their formats are both limited to a rectangle that is horizontally oriented. The **horizontal line** is a reflection of the line that defines the width of the frame. Lines that mirror the horizon serve to underline the expanse of the rectangle. They can also create two or more rectangles within the frame. This compositional approach is often found in westerns, where man's vertical stance is seen against the backdrop of an expansive horizon.

Potemkin

Vertical lines are reflections of the sides of the frame. They are found in shots or frames that feature a figure against a field, buildings against the sky, or any other element that reaches up in defiance of gravity.

The **diagonal line** splits the frame into triangles. It also serves to move the eye in a direction that leads outside the frame. This can be used to create dynamic motion from one shot to the next as well as movement within the single frame itself. The diagonal approach supports asymmetry and imbalance in the frame.

Potemkin

M

Circles, Squares, Triangles, and More

Sometimes a simple geometric shape serves as the structuring element of a shot. Of course, every shot starts with the inescapable rectangle of the frame. The horizontal orientation is a given, no matter which aspect ratio is being utilized. What we sculpt inside that rectangle is another matter. In the three adjacent frames you can observe familiar shapes that offer strong, simple solutions to structuring the space inside the borders of a rectangular frame.

Triangles   *Potemkin*

Squares   *M*

Circles   *Golddiggers of '33*

139

CONTRAST, TEXTURE, AND OTHER ELEMENTS OF THE IMAGE

There are also some subtler methods of manipulating the eye aside from the obvious graphic structure of the frame. The texture of each form and the contrast between their values can express something about the world and the characters that inhabit the space and the time of the story. These elements are not as easily noticed by the audience but can contribute to the overall "read" of the picture.

Contrast

Contrast cannot exist without comparing one part of a frame to another. The type of contrast that this section refers to is one that is created by the juxtaposition of areas of different **value**. Value is the relative lightness or darkness of a color or a tone.

10 % gray
25% gray
50% gray
75% gray
100% black

Contrast is often measured in terms of its percentage of relative darkness. Black is expressed as 100% and white as 0% so that a middle gray can be called a 45-55% value of gray. Values are not just used in black-and-white situations. Each color or hue has its own value translation, or relative lightness or darkness that can be expressed in terms of value.

The term "high contrast" refers to the use of a large spread of values within the frame, so that you will see both deep blacks and bright, sparkling whites within the same scene. A "low contrast" composition uses a limited spread of values, perhaps only 40% of the possible array of lights and darks.

The eye interprets darker values as receding in space and lighter ones as coming forward in the picture plane. Observe the frames to the right to see

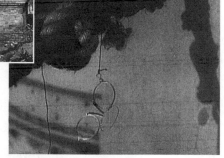

how your attention moves through the space in these examples of high and low contrast compositions.

Potemkin

Texture

We tend to think of texture as something that is felt through the skin, an element of our sense of touch, not of sight. Although the world of images is flat, there are a variety of ways to add texture to a shot. The most all-encompassing is through the choice of different film stocks and lenses. It is beyond the scope of this volume to cover all the possibilities in this area, but a general understanding of grain and depth of field can be useful for anyone involved in creating images on film and video.

Texture can also be seen in the surfaces of nubby fabric, plastered walls, and the shiny chrome of a 1950s Chevy. There are times when an abstract shot of a broken-down wall or a rain-slicked street will tell the viewer something about the story that no line of dialogue or shot of action can manage to do.

Alexander Nevsky

Color

A spot of color in a gray landscape draws the eye to it regardless of its placement or scale. This powerful element of composition is so complex that it evades a thorough treatment in this book. Let it suffice to say that color is an element of composition that is uniquely powerful and subtle at the same time. There are many excellent essays that take on this topic; a list of recommended sources will be found in the Bibliography (page 219).

SUMMARY

This chapter has covered some of the most common strategies for structuring the frame. They are not mutually exclusive. Many frames use a combination of these elements and function beautifully in terms of aesthetics and narrative.

Of course, there are scripts that don't need such tightly composed shots. The liberal use of hand-held shooting, as seen in John Cassavetes's *A Woman Under the Influence* (1974), Woody Allen's *Husbands and Wives* (1992), Lars von Trier's *Breaking the Waves* (1996), and in innumerable films shot in the "cinema verite" style, precludes the necessity of heavy preproduction visualization. In fact, to do so would be counter-productive to telling those particular stories.

The script usually leads the way but story can be subsumed by style. In other words, there is a delicate balance between the form of the composition and the content of the story. Use these tools with precision, but not necessarily in every frame or circumstance. Each decision carries the weight of the history of making pictures — perhaps a daunting challenge, but one that can also inspire new ways of seeing and telling great stories.

Exercise: Composition
Griding the Screen and Painting the Frame

• Chose a film that you admire, but have not had a great deal of time to observe. (The film can be in color or B&W, but I recommend starting with a film that is black and white; with a gray scale image there are fewer elements to contend with, and fewer materials to assemble.)

• Stretch a piece of clear acetate over the screen of your television or monitor and secure it with tape on all sides. Then, with a chisel tip black marker, draw two diagonal lines that extend to each corner of the film frame. Where these cross in the center, draw vertical and horizontal lines that bisect the screen. (Remember that if you are watching a film that is being presented in a letterbox format, you need to draw the diagonals to that proportion, *not* to the corners of the screen.)

• Watch the film and observe the composition of each shot with reference to the lines on the screen. (It helps to have the volume on low.)

• Make note of the shots that interest you in terms of their visual structure. Then take three pieces of illustration board that have been cut to the aspect ratio of your film. I recommend using 9" by 16.5" for the 1.85 ratio or the equivalent for other ratios. Paint gray scale interpretations of the compositions of your chosen shots. You don't need to slavishly try to copy the frames. Allow yourself some creative freedom and have fun.

Example of grided screen   *Potemkin*

Losing it, Briefly

There are times when the extremely demanding hours of production bring
out less than admirable behavior. The trick is to recover with grace and
keep moving ahead. I was working on a shoot that was long on both hours
and creativity. This being a combination that I eagerly pursue, I was
pleased to be on the set late one night when a strange situation
developed. It was 2 AM and we'd been shooting for hours, trying to finish
a large crowd scene set in a hotel lobby. We were preparing for a stunt
where someone would crash through one of the hotel's plate glass windows.
Extras were milling about the lobby, drinking coffee and chatting quietly
while the crew set up the next shot. It was my turn to collect all the
craft service Styrofoam cups from the cast and extras on the set.

I approached a group of people sitting on a bench that was in the middle
of the shot and asked them to please hand over their cups. One person in
the group was using his cup as an ashtray and he refused to hand it to
me. O.K, it was late and everyone tired, bored, and hungry, but the
cameras were now about to roll. I asked again and the guy took the cup
and hid it behind his back. Foolishly, I took the bait and reached behind
him to nab it. He then decided to give it to me, and proceeded to crush
the cup, butts and all, against my head.

This kind of rough play tends to escalate quickly. I hauled back and
slapped him on the face and was rewarded with a kick to my shin. The
crowd drew back, anticipating a real battle. I stand barely 5'3" and
have no martial arts training, so I started screaming for reinforcements.
The producer heard my cry and as he walked over I demanded that the
hooligan be removed from the set.

It was then that I was informed that I had just struck an actor. Not a
major one, but a necessary one, nonetheless. Embarrassed but not ashamed,
I retreated to the relative calm of an adjacent room that the art
department was using as a storage area. I was telling my side of the
story to the crew when the producer came in and informed us that the
actor was now refusing to work until he received an apology. Still hot
with the passion of the fight, I refused. I was reminded that in this
circumstance we needed to 'defer to talent.' I suggested that if that
were the case, the actor should get down on his knees to me.

I was pissed. I had been roughed up in the course of performing my on-
set duties and an apology was not forthcoming. But nothing was getting
accomplished. We had a hundred extras waiting around and it was near 3 in
the morning. Time to get off it. OK, I told him, I'll handle it. I went
back to the set and approached my grumbling opponent. He sneered at me
as I knelt by his side. I don't remember exactly what I said, but a few
minutes later we shook hands and he went back to work. People working
under high pressure and on little sleep can exhibit strange behavior.
Sometimes it becomes necessary to remind yourself that it's only a movie.

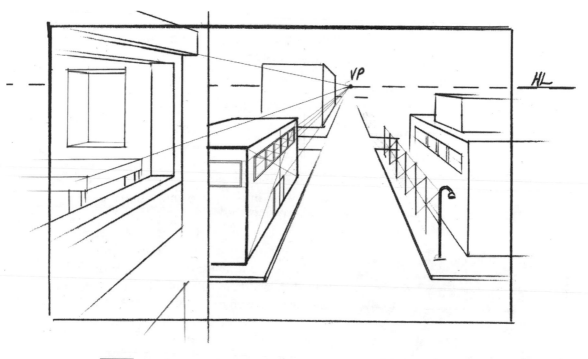

7 Perspective

"...any person of sound mind can learn to draw; the probability is the same for learning to read."

Betty Edwards
Drawing on the Artist Within

An Introduction to Perspective

Perspective: from the Latin "prospectus," *to look forward*

Why perspective?

Perspective is a topic that rarely surfaces when talking about film, but it is crucial to any discussion about translating the three-dimensional world into the two-dimensional plane of the film frame.

The world that surrounds us is one of three dimensions. The room you are sitting in is defined by width, length, and height. A piece of paper or strip of film has only two dimensions that are used for the image that rests upon it. In order to refer to the three dimensions of space on a two-dimensional surface, we need a drawing convention, an illusion that will trick the eye into thinking that the flat image has depth. Western art has developed a system of technical perspective that is invaluable to creating accurate storyboards; this chapter will spend some time helping you to become familiar with this drawing system.

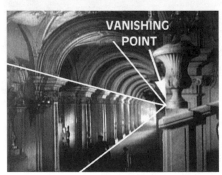

VANISHING POINT

In perspective, the parallel lines that define an image's depth converge to a spot called the vanishing point. In this chapter you will **learn how to place your camera position to correspond with your vanishing points, so your sketch will accurately reflect your intended shot.** There is perhaps no better way to immediately improve your ability to communicate about the visual world than to learn this method of representation.

The prospect of learning this new material may seem daunting to some of you. I can only tell you that I have seen remarkable progress in just a few hours from students who walk into classes and workshops with little or no previous drawing experience. The perspective drawing system in this book has been developed using the architectural approach as a starting point, but has been substantially simplified for the benefit of filmmakers and professionals in related fields.

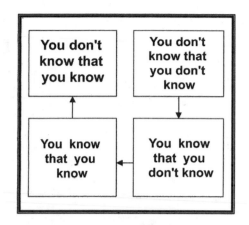

How we learn: A diagram

Examples of student progress

before   after

before   after

upper images: Nick Hill
lower images: Michael Bertucci

PERSPECTIVE IN YOUR ENVIRONMENT

The room you are sitting in is most likely constructed from walls that are at 90-degree angles to each other. If you're sitting at a table, the same is probably true for the relationship of its top and legs. Many if not most of the man-made objects in our environment are built on the right angle. It is easy to join together and creates strength in both lateral and vertical directions.

In a cube we have three sets of facets which correspond to the height, depth, and length of three-dimensional space. When one or more of these facets are parallel to one side of our picture plane, then only the remaining sides will require vanishing points for the lines that define them in pictorial space. Perspective drawing is based on the relationship of the sets of parallel faces that result in objects built on right angles.

When looking at a cube straight-on, the top of the cube is parallel to the top edge of your imaginary picture plane. The sides of the cube are parallel to the vertical edges. Only the planes that describe the depth of the cube are not in a parallel relationship with your picture plane. Those are the edges that need a vanishing point to describe the illusion of depth in the frame.

If we now rotate that cube so that the front plane is on a 45-degree angle to the picture plane, then that plane as well as the previous plane needs vanishing points.

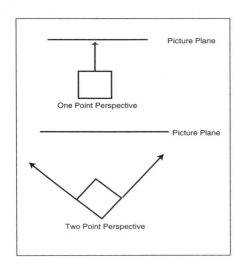

A = vertical lines
B = horizontal lines
C = needs vanishing pt!

Picture Plane

One Point Perspective

Picture Plane

Two Point Perspective

Perspective

Vocabulary

Station point: The position of the observer. The placement of the camera. This position can be plotted in the overhead diagram.

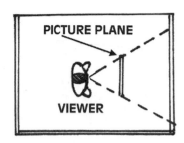

Picture plane: An imaginary plane set at a 90-degree angle to the observer, onto which the image of the scene is projected.

Imagine that you are holding a rectangular sheet of Plexiglas straight out in front of your body, and you are gazing through it at the world. That rectangle is acting as the picture plane. It is the two-dimensional surface that acts as projection screen for the three-dimensional world.

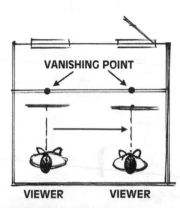

Horizon line: An imaginary line that is determined by the height of the camera or the observer of a scene.

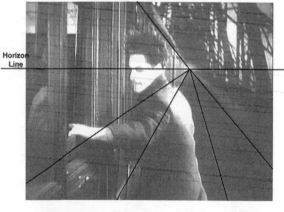

Vanishing point: A point which lies on the horizon and acts as a guide for the plotting of lines and planes that describe depth in the drawing.

Plan view (schematic): The layout of a scene from overhead. This is a diagram, not a drawing, of an overhead view of the set. Often used to situate camera positions within the sets. The plan view, or schematic, is used in perspective to plot the station point (camera position) in relation to the set pieces that are to be rendered.

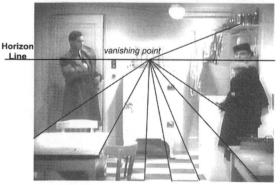

Cone of vision (Field of view): The perimeter of the observer's vision. In film, the cone of vision, also called "field of view," is limited by the aspect ratio of the frame. This field of view shifts according to the length of the lens used for the shot. The longer the lens, the narrower the cone of vision.

1 pt = frontal shots, straight-on down street directly at wall of room

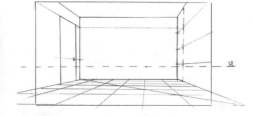

One-point perspective: The situation of needing only one vanishing point to describe depth in a scene. When we are looking at a cube straight-on, the top and the bottom planes of that cube will be parallel to the top and the bottom of the picture plane. The sides of the cube will be parallel to the vertical edges of the picture plane. Those planes will be described by lines that are horizontal and vertical. Only the planes that give the cube its depth will need to be described by lines that converge. These lines will converge at the vanishing point.

When to use one-point perspective
This system of perspective is used for sketching shots that are seen from frontal angles. The camera is placed straight-on to the back wall in interior shots and looks straight onto a building or down the street in exterior shots.

Two-point perspective: This is used in situations when two vanishing points are needed to communicate depth — as in when the cube is placed at an angle to the observer and the only set of planes that is parallel to the picture plane are the vertical ones. In this orientation, both sides of the cube are angled away from the observer and each set of lines that describe those sides will need its own vanishing point.

2 pt = 3/4 ∢ shots
raking angles
oblique angles

When to use two-point perspective

When you are setting up an interior shot that looks into a room corner or is at a raking angle (a position that is not square) in relation to the walls of the room, you will be using a two-point setup. Each wall will need its own vanishing point, as they are both carving the depth of the room space.

In exterior scenes, a camera that is viewing a building or street scene from a 3/4 angle will create a need for two vanishing points in your drawing.

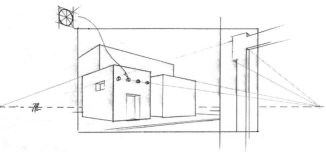

Three-point perspective: A system used when the object has no faces that are parallel to the picture plane. The vertical lines as well as the lines parallel to the floor are drawn to vanishing points.

3 pt = • helicopter shots
• worm's eye view

When to use three-point perspective

Usually for very high or low shots, when you need to convey the height of an object or building which is receding into the distance.

THE PENCIL HITS THE PAPER

The next section will cover the use of the perspective system in sketching storyboard imagery. It will cover both one- and two-point perspective systems and their application in creating a sketch that takes into account the camera height and position relative to the set and characters.

Drawing a Cube in One-point Perspective

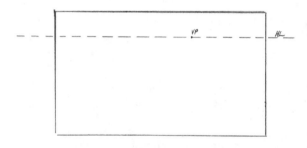

Start by making a frame on your paper. Using a 6" by 10 1/2" frame will give you an approximation of the 1.85 aspect ratio that is used as a standard in American projection projects. After completing your frame select a camera height by placing your horizon line some distance between the top and bottom edge of the frame. Start with selecting a high camera and draw a light line 1/4 of the way down from the top of the frame. The horizon line will be a horizontal line, unless the shot is set at a canted angle.

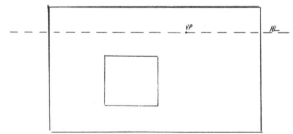

Once the horizon line is set, choose a position for the vanishing point. In one-point perspective, the vanishing point will always be on the horizon, equidistant from the sides of the frame.

Next, draw the front face of the box as a regular square. Remember that any face of the cube that is parallel to the top and the bottom of the frame can be drawn with vertical and horizontal lines. Only the faces that describe the depth of the cube will need a vanishing point as a guide.

Now that you have the front face of the cube, use the vanishing point to determine the angle of the sides and the top face of the cube. Use the vanishing point as a pivot and draw light lines from the corners of the front face back towards the horizon. These lines are "imaginary" and by drawing them to the horizon they have an infinite distance.

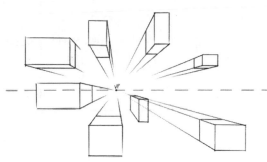

To finish off the cube, pass a vertical line through the bottom and the middle lines that you have just drawn. Where that line touches the top of the box, draw a horizontal line over to describe the back edge of your cube.

Transforming the Box into an Exterior Street Scene

Once you have drawn this cube in perspective, begin to expand the drawing into a high-angle street scene. The box can be easily made into a building by adding doors, windows, and other architectural details.

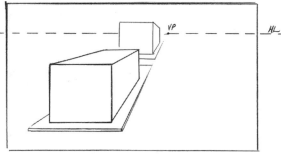

Any doors or windows that appear on a front face (a regular rectangle) will be drawn with vertical and horizontal lines. Any details added to the planes that have been drawn using the vanishing points will also use those points to determine the angles of their upper and lower edges.

Adding streets is easy. Imagine that they are flat planes, like the bottoms of unfinished cubes, that create a grid around your cube-buildings. By using horizontal lines to send the streets across the frame and lines that aim toward the vanishing point to send the streets back into the depth of the drawing, you can create a scene that has a look of solid reality about it.

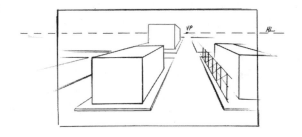

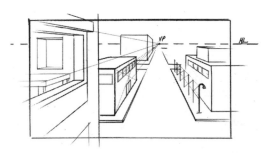

When you want to give those streets a curb, use a vertical line to drop down a small distance and then draw two more lines, one across the frame and another into the depth by way of the vanishing point.

Now have some fun. Add in buildings across the street, further back in the scene, and behind the ones in the foreground. Add a row of trees or telephone poles that diminish in height as they approach the vanishing point. Draw a box in above the horizon line and see what happens.

Measuring Depth in One-point Perspective Space

You can measure the depth of your object by the "eyeball" method and approximate the back edge by taking into consideration the decreasing size of the object's face as it recedes in space. Or, there is a method that allows you to use diagonal lines as guides to measure equal distances into the distance.

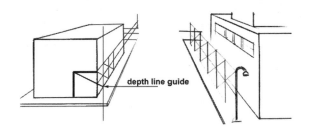

depth line guide

Begin by bisecting a vertical line of your box with a small mark. Pass a line from the opposite corner of the cube through that mark, and continue on until it crosses the bottom edge of a side. Where the two lines intersect, draw a vertical line and you will have drawn a box that is equal in measurement across the front and the sides.

One-point Perspective Interiors

Now that you have the tools to draw boxes from the outside, let's go inside the box and draw the interior of a bedroom set.

Draw a frame as you did at the beginning of the last drawing. The first decision to make on the interior plan is to decide how much of the back wall is visible in the shot. If you are shooting down a long corridor, the back wall might appear as a small vertically oriented rectangle. If we are in a ballroom, then the back wall might be represented as a long, horizontal rectangle.

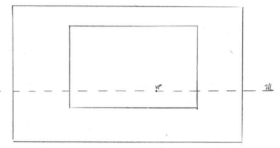

Since the camera's height will determine the height of the horizon line, the back wall must be drawn in before the horizon line is set. Choose a height for your camera and draw in the horizon as a horizontal line crossing through the back wall.

If the horizon line is drawn in above the back wall, that would signify a camera that is above the height of the set walls. There are some circumstances where this would be appropriate, but most situations call for the camera to be inside the room.

Student example by Jennifer Nies

The rear wall of the room does not need to be centered in the frame. The camera can be

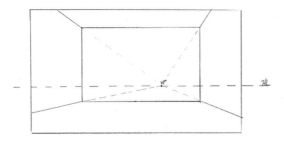

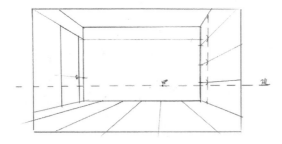

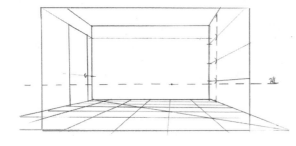

closer to either side wall if desired, but in any case the vanishing point will be centered in the frame.

Mark the vanishing point on the horizon line and draw the lines that will delineate your walls, floor, and ceiling, passing each line through a corner of the rear wall and using the vanishing point as a guide to its angle.

Once the walls are set, then begin to add the details of the room: a door, a couple of windows, and perhaps a floor rug. Remember as you move around the room that any detail appearing on a wall that is drawn as a rectangle will also appear as a rectangle. Any detail appearing on a wall that is drawn to the vanishing point will also use the vanishing point to determine its top and bottom edges.

Adding Furniture to the Interior Scene

Just as the truck in the exterior scene was carved out of a box, the same method can be used to create furniture for the bedroom (or any other interior scene). To begin, locate the position of the bed by drawing a rectangle on the floor, the "footprint" of the object. To work in scale, we can apply the technique that we used in the previous example to work out the measurement of the side walls.

Mark out equal divisions on the horizontal floor line. Then use the vanishing point to extend them with light lines into the room.

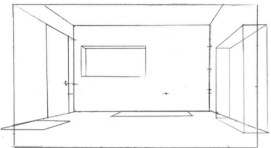

Draw a square in the corner of the back wall and bisect the side of the square that lies on the floor. Then pass a line through that mark from the vanishing point and out into the floor space. Where that line crosses each light line, you can draw a horizontal. Notice that the space between those lines increases as you move farther out into the room. Although that is the case, the lines represent equal distances along the floor. You can use this technique to scale the objects that you place in the room.

Once the bed's footprint is in place, raise one corner of it using a vertical line. Use the height of your back wall as a measure to make sure that the bed is in scale with the rest of the room. Once the height is set, then complete the cube. Make it into a bed by adding boxes on top with rounded edges that will become pillows and softening the lines of the large box to give it the visual feel of a mattress and bedding.

Chairs, Bookcases, Etc.

A slightly more complex form is the upholstered chair. Again, start with a footprint to give you the location of the chair in the room. Draw the facing plane first using vertical and horizontal lines. Then use the vanishing point to extend those lines to the back of the cube. As you do this, think of carving the space of the box. Look over the following examples of familiar furniture shapes that can be carved from cubes.

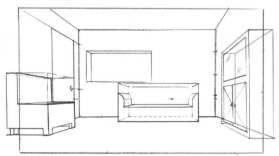

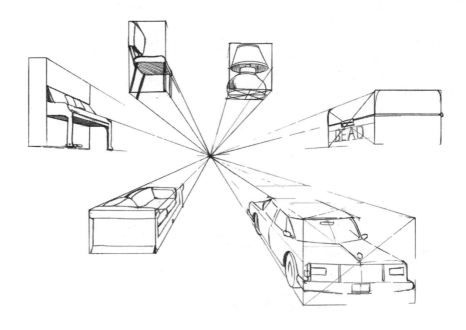

Circles in Perspective

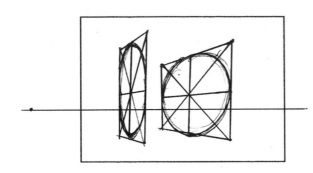

Let's say that you have a hanging, cylindrical lamp on your set. Unless you are looking straight at the underside of the cylinder, the circle will appear as an ellipse when you draw it in perspective. In order to find the correct shape for the circular edge, first construct a square in perspective at the level of the lamp-shade. Then connect the opposite corners with straight lines. This will give you the center of your ellipse. Using the midpoint, draw two lines that bisect the rectangle and are either parallel to the edges or vanishing to the horizon. These four lines will touch the polygon at eight points. Now use these points as a guide to drawing the ellipse.

Two-point Perspective

The next point of view is that of looking into a corner of a room or at a building at a 3/4 angle. In this situation, you need two vanishing points for the two sets of planes that describe the depth of the space. First, we will set up a high, wide shot of a city street.

Draw a frame as you did in the last exercise. A 9" by 16" rectangle will give you a frame with an aspect ratio that approximates the American projection standard of 1.85. The horizon line will signify the height of the camera, so draw a horizontal line passing through the upper third and extending out to the sides of the frame. That is the line that the vanishing points will be drawn on.

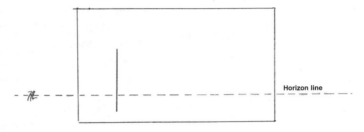

Horizon line

Here's where the simple sketch method is different from the architecturally precise one. In an architectural perspective drawing, an artist will draw out the setting on a plan view or overhead drawing. Then each point on this overhead is carried out to the picture plane, drawn up into an elevation, and then finally taken back to the vanishing points in order to finish the perspective sketch. This is a time-consuming if visually precise way of rendering the scene.

We are going to skip a few steps. This will require you to take a few matters on trust, but the ends should justify these reduced means.

How to Find the Vanishing Points in Two-Point Perspective

The distance between the two vanishing points is determined by the length of the camera's lens and its distance from the subject. Changing lenses is tantamount to changing the observer's distance from what he or she is looking at as well. As the lens length changes — i.e., gets wider — the picture plane moves further away from the subject of the shot. As this happens the vanishing points spread out further and further. If the lens length grows longer, then the picture plane moves in.

If we dispense with the steps of drawing an overhead and plotting the points of the set onto an elevation, then we need a quick way of determining the placement of the vanishing points by eye. The suggested placement is one-half a frame's distance outside the frame on either side for a natural, 50 mm lens length appearance.

You will find that if you decrease this space and place the points next to the frame, you will end up with a drawing in which the objects begin to show distortion as they near the vanishing points. This distortion would be similar to what you would find if you were shooting with an 18 mm lens.

The distance between the two vanishing points is relative to the distance of the picture plane from the object. The points can be equidistant from the frame, which describes an object that is angled 45 degrees to the picture plane.

When the angle of the object changes, the vanishing points move along the horizon line so that one or the other is closer and the other is further away, keeping the same relative distance as they move.

THE LONGER THE LENS, THE FARTHER OUT FROM THE FRAME THE VANISHING POINTS WILL APPEAR.

Drawing a Box in Two-point Perspective, Exterior Scene

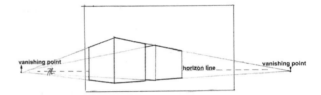

After you draw a frame choose a height for the camera. Lay in the horizon line, and for a natural-looking image, place the vanishing points approximately one half a frame's width outside the frame. This will keep the angles of the drawing from getting too severe, which can happen when the points are drawn too close to the frame. Think of the distortion that an 18 mm lens can create when shooting objects close-up.

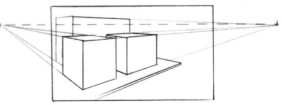

Once the vanishing points are in place, draw in a vertical line that will stand for the height of the box on the edge that is closest to the camera. Now use the vanishing points to draw in the sides and the top of the box. With this method, you will "eyeball" the distance to the back edge of the object.

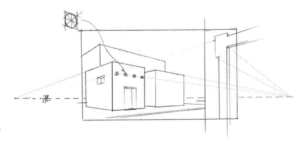

161

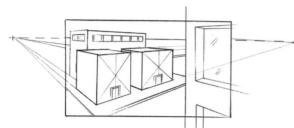

Once you have the two-point perspective cube drawn, enlarge the image so that you have another street scene. Try giving it some character, like an old-style street out of a western or a futuristic scene from the year 2300.

Try drawing the same street using a higher camera. Just place the horizon line near the top of the frame. Use the same vanishing point and vertical start lines and start sketching.

Two-point Perspective Interiors

You will use this approach when you are setting up a shot that is looking into a corner of a room. It also is known as a 3/4 angle or raking shot.

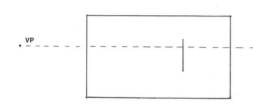

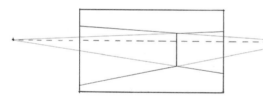

Start with a horizontal frame and visualize how far you are from the back wall or the corner of the space. As in the interior of the one-point perspective room, the back wall line needs to be drawn in before the horizon line is set. If you are looking deep into a large space, the line might cover only a fraction of the height of the frame. If you are in a smaller room, the line will be longer.

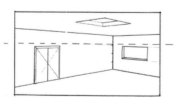

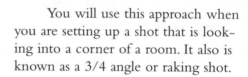

Place a vertical line in your frame and decide the height of the camera by drawing a horizon line through the frame. Place the two vanishing points on the horizon line, outside the frame itself. Now draw the lines that will describe the ceiling, floor, and walls. Use the vanishing points as pivots and draw *the left wall using the right vanishing point and the right wall using the left one.* This can be tricky to remember, but in two–point perspective you only use the right vanishing point to draw right-sided planes when you are drawing the outside of a box. When you are inside the box, you flip the orientation and use the *opposite* vanishing point.

This procedure may seem strange at first, but after drawing a few interiors it will become second nature. Once the walls are drawn in, begin to furnish the room. Pop in a couple of windows, a door, and try a fireplace. Add a table, some chairs, and place a couple of standing figures in the scene. You can use the vanishing points to scale the figures in the space.

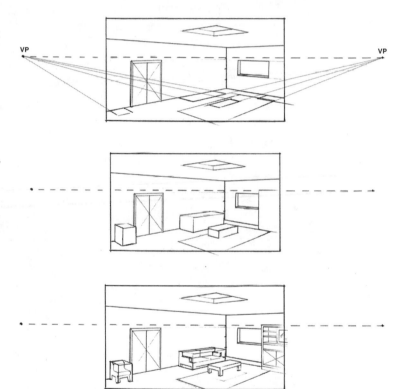

Exercise

Once you have gone through the proceeding material, try to render this short shot list using the correct version of perspective and the appropriate horizon line. A student example is provided for reference.

1. Exterior day, western town. High angle, frontal shot of a small 19th century town. A wagon lies abandoned in the street.
2. Full shot of the saloon doors, a man waits to come through. Eyelevel raking angle.
3. ECU of man's eyes, frontal.
4. Straight-on wide shot, eye-level of the front of saloon. Track left to follow man over to hotel.

Student example

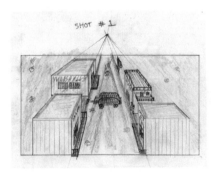

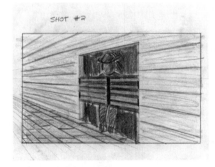

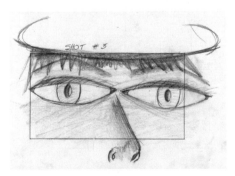

drawings: Eric Thompson

BEYOND THE BOX

This chapter has offered some bare-bones techniques on adding space to your sketches. It is meant as a tool for those writers and directors who need a simple visual language to communicate their shot ideas. For additional information on perspective, please refer to the excellent sources in the Bibliography (page 219) and consider taking a short class in linear perspective at your local community college or art academy.

Perspective sketch: Leo Kuter
production designer: *Key Largo*, *Rio Bravo*

Portfolio on the Loose

Two years after I arrived in Los Angeles, I had managed to put together enough work to fill a good-sized portfolio. This included storyboards, production sketches, and set photos from the films that I had decorated. I decided that it was time to introduce myself to a larger community of art directors and production designers. To this end, I invested in a beautiful leather-edged case with large plastic-covered pages inside. I made up captions, typed up a new resume and had large prints made of all my best set shots.

I called up the art directors I had already worked with and asked for the names of other art directors who might be looking to expand their crews. I set up seven or eight meetings over the course of two weeks and was set to begin the interview process when I decided to go downtown to show my new book to a friend. We were going to have dinner and since the portfolio was large and heavy and I was running late, I locked it in the trunk of my car. We finished about 9:30 and walked back to the lot. It was one of the outdoor lots common to downtown Los Angeles. The attendant had already gone home. We reached the car and I popped the lock. I will always remember the sight of that empty trunk. I had trouble breathing as I tried to take in what had happened. I even checked to see if I was dreaming. No such luck; the portfolio was gone. And this was not just my Los Angeles work, but photos of sets I had designed in New York, original set illustrations...everything.

Mildly stated, I was very upset. We began to comb the area looking in every dumpster for a three-block radius. I called the police and made a report, but they weren't helpful. I could only hope that whomever had the case would dump the contents and they would be recovered. But nothing ever turned up. And I had interviews with some of the top designers in town starting the next day and nothing to show.

When I returned home I began to comb through the "reject" pile for some photos and storyboards that I could cobble into a presentation format. I was desperate, just this side of defeated at the daunting task of redoing all my work, but between calls to coworkers for replacement photos and long hours at the drawing table, I managed to create a "portfolio version 2.0," which was in some ways better than its predecessor. Thereafter I vowed to never leave the portfolio in my car, never put original work in the book, and always have copies made of my drawings. I also realized that even when my most "valuable" professional possession was taken from me I was able to go to my interviews and make a convincing presentation. They were hiring me, not my portfolio. In subsequent years I insisted, whenever possible, to meet with prospective employers personally, and not just leave a portfolio as some requested. Even if it was just to shake hands and say hello, there is power in connecting a person to the portfolio.

8 Figure Notation

"On the first film I directed, I made drawings. I wanted to be very sure. I was uncertain of myself as far as the camera was concerned and I wanted to be sure not to fumble, not to get lost in the mechanical aspects of making a film. So I made drawings of every set-up..."

John Huston, *Hollywood Voices*
director: *The Maltese Falcon, The African Queen*

The Human Form

8

"Don't try to do a complete drawing all at once. Spend all the time you can doodling with stick figures. They're the easiest way for you to get the action and position that you want for your characters."

Stan Lee
How to Draw Comics the Marvel Way

This chapter will concentrate on the development of figure notation. The human figure is perhaps the most common element in film composition. Whether the shot is a close-up, a long shot, or a full-figure, chances are that there will be a human form somewhere inside the frame. Some of you will approach this challenge with little or no figure drawing experience. Others, myself included, come from a background in fine art and are accustomed to referring to live models as we draw. For those with limited or no drawing experience, this chapter will take you through some simple steps that will improve your ability to render natural-looking figures. For artists accustomed to using live models, the information will guide you toward simplifying your notion of the human body so that you can quickly render human forms using a simple internalized model instead of a complex live figure.

Our bodies are composed of over 200 bones and hundreds more muscles. Besides these basic biological traits, our forms carry marks of personality, gender, ethnicity, and individual history. That makes the human figure one of the most complex forms to render in a natural-looking manner.

"For *Duel* the entire movie was story-boarded. I think that when you make an action film, especially a road picture, it's the best way to work, because it's very hard to pick up a script and sift through five hundred words of prose and then commit them to memory....I felt that breaking the picture up and mapping it out would be easier for me."

Steven Spielberg
director: *Jaws, E.T., Schindler's List*

That said, the director or writer who is using storyboards to help visualize his or her project needs to concentrate only on some of the fundamentals of the form.

Main Elements of Figure Communication:

- **SCALE**
- **PROPORTION**
- **GESTURE**
- **THREE-DIMENSIONAL FORM (various approaches)**
- **Skeletal**
- **Simple geometric shapes**
- **Stacked ellipses**

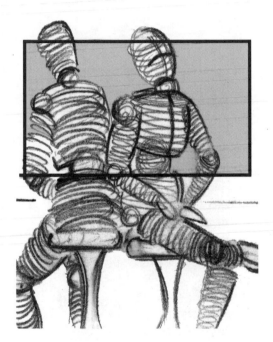

The fine artist and the illustrator have a different challenge. For them, the process involves simplifying a form they already understand in terms of its deep complexities. To accommodate the storyboard format, the network of interlaced shapes that make up the head, torso, and extremities of a human form will now need to be rendered on a relatively small scale, often no larger than 3" by 5". In addition, the presentation of light and shadow needs to be accomplished as quickly and accurately as possible.

Simplified Forms

Sometimes a storyboard artist will get location or set model photos to use as reference, but most of the time you will find yourself working from overhead diagrams and shot descriptions. Many artists new to storyboarding find they have to develop a revised set of rendering skills that focus on mentally designing each shot before they begin to visualize it on paper.

When I came into the film industry I had been working as a set designer for theater and as an artist who specialized in portraiture. When I began to work as a storyboard artist it took me well over a year to internalize a generic human that I could call forth from my mind at will, having no external imagery for reference.

The first step for me was to acquire a 12" high mannequin with moveable limbs. These can be found in most art and graphic supply stores. They usually are built with simple wooden shapes, an egg-like form for the head, a sphere for the neck pivot, a rounded trapezoid for the torso, and tapered cylinders for the arms and legs. There are no articulated fingers or facial features, just the basics.

The limbs, head, and torso are linked by a spring mechanism that allows you to pose the figure, and then lets the "body" maintain that shape after you release the limbs. By using an aspect ratio cutout, you can arrange the mannequin so that you can see the gesture of the figure in whichever scale you desire. You now have a visual reference from which to build your drawing.

This approach may sound time-consuming, but it's actually fun. There is a lovely element of play to this that will make the time pass quickly. Also, many people experience a higher level of achievement with a short amount of practice using this tool.

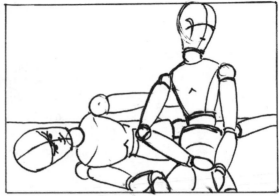

You cannot over-estimate the importance of play in this process. Many of you stopped drawing, cut yourselves off from expressing the visual world, when your internal criticisms became too severe. Small children have a universal love of painting and drawing. It is inbred, just as the need to speak and to write comes with the desire to communicate about the world. Some of you will now be opening yourselves up to an ancient manner of expression. In the history of "scripting" the image pre-dates the word.

In the preliminary storyboard image, remember:

- **Gesture Before Detail**
- **Three-Dimensional Figure in Space**
- **Simple Animation of Facial Expressions**

The Figure

The focus here will be on three ways to quickly sketch the figure and communicate its gestures in space. Skeletons are the next step up from the beginner's stick-figure rendition of the human body. They can be created from some simple building blocks that are far easier to put together than a fully-clothed figure.

The next step up might be creating human forms from simple geometric shapes, such as cylinders and cubes. Stacked in proportion, this figure can be rotated and sketched more easily from memory than a true anatomical version.

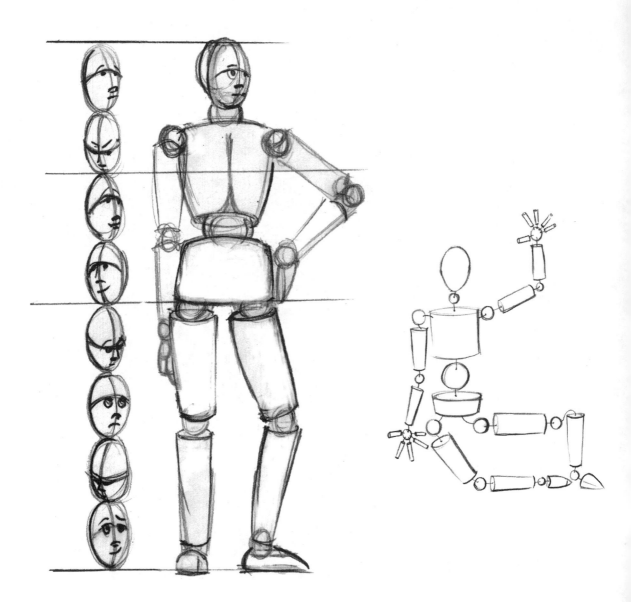

Stacked ellipses, which can be sketched as unbroken spirals, can also be helpful in getting the figure into three dimensions. Remember, you are attempting to *refer* to human movement and positioning, not faithfully *reproduce* it.

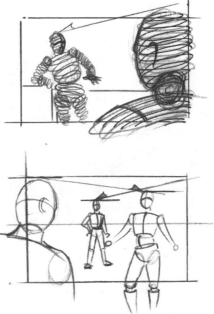

Use vanishing points to line up the tops of heads.

Try sketching mannequins in various positions.

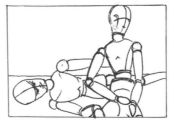

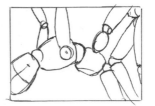

175

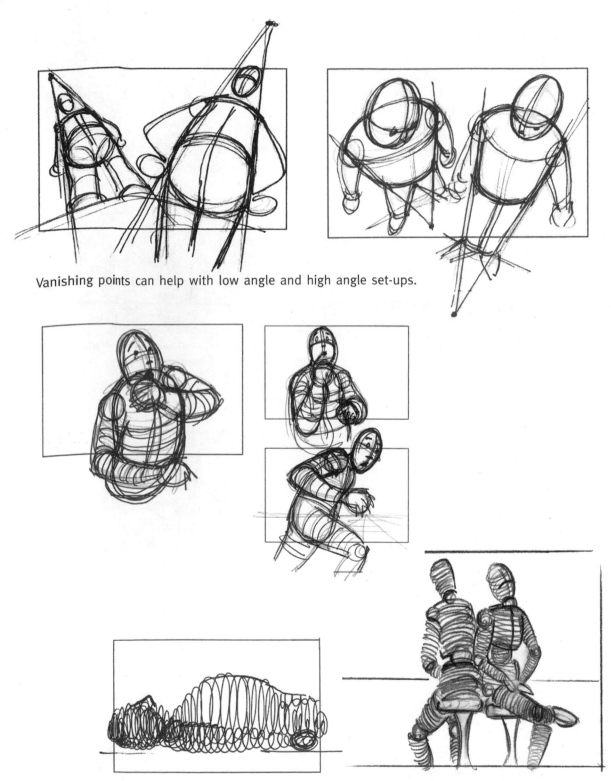

Vanishing points can help with low angle and high angle set-ups.

The Head

It's said that as we age, our face shows the life we have lived. Of all the parts that make up our bodies, the head has attracted the most attention. It is the site of the "windows to our souls," the plane on which our expressions reflect our emotional lives. It can communicate our feelings, which are at times a counterpoint to our words.

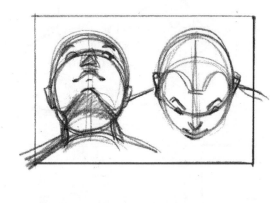

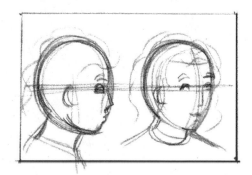

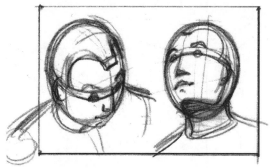

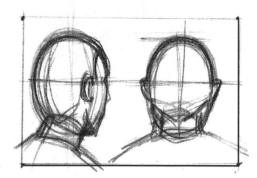

Let's start with the egg. An egg on end, with the thicker end toward the sky, is a good place to start in the rendering of a head.

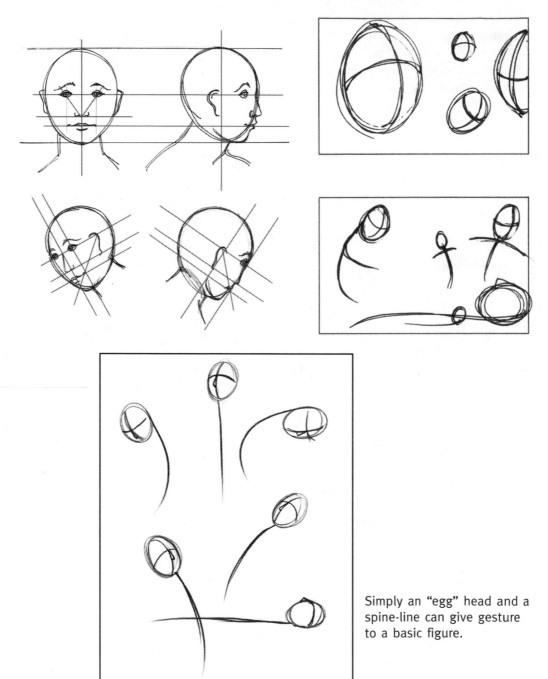

Simply an "egg" head and a spine-line can give gesture to a basic figure.

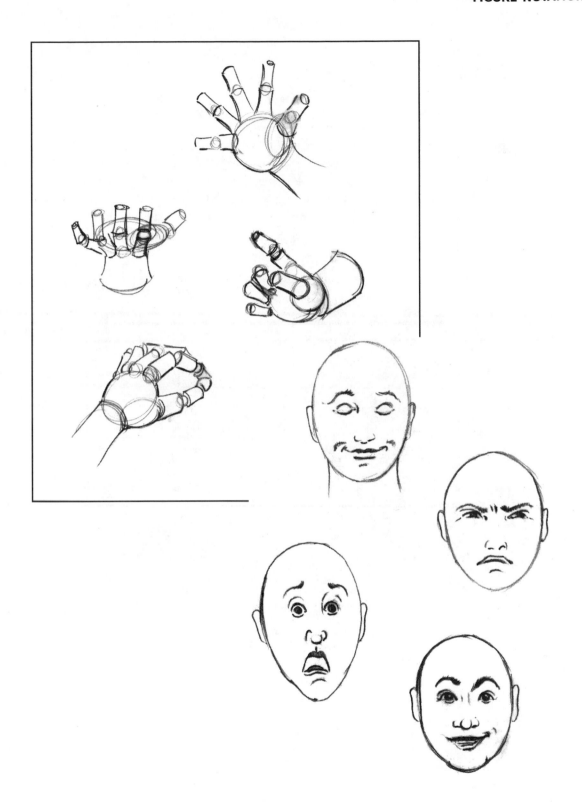

Summary

The important thing to remember is that **this process needs to focus on experimentation, not "success" and "failure"** as viewed through the comparison of your drawings to the art of professional illustrators. As directors and writers you are looking for a shorthand style to effectively communicate your ideas on blocking and composition. It's not that you "can't draw" or that you are missing some "talent" that other people seem to be born with. It's just that you need to sharpen a skill which has been long dormant.

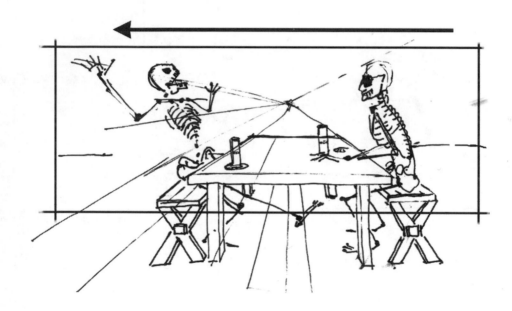

See What You Can Come Up With

I was hired to storyboard a feature for a first-
time director. He had worked in music videos and
commercials and had a great visual flair. I arrived
for our first meeting and was asked to wait outside
his office because he was busy interviewing
designers. I read the newspapers. I went for
coffee. His assistant apologized, and I went to
lunch. That afternoon he was busy with casting.
Finally he had a break in his schedule and I was
offered a seat across from his desk. He handed me a
script and asked me to look at couple of scenes and
get back to him when I had something for him to
look at. No conversation, no advice guidance of any
kind. We worked together in this way for a few
weeks. I would stop by to drop off drawings and get
a new assignment. He would glance at the work and
run off for another casting session. I had a good
time drawing up the boards, but never made much of
a connection with the director or figured out how
he was planning to use the information. When I saw
the completed film, it was clear that he didn't use
the boards at all.

People use the boards in many ways. Sometimes they
are a way to involve another sensibility into the
visual mix. Sometimes they are created just to
satisfy the demands of an off-site producing
organization. It's a good idea to determine where
the boards are heading and what purpose they will
be put to before you start the process.

drawing: Anton Grot
production designer: *LIttle Caesar*,
Gold Diggers of 1933, *Mildred Pierce*

9 Getting a Gig

"Artists need a full, convertible portfolio.
Producers and directors can have tunnel-vision
when it comes to visualizing their project. Artists
can be typecast just like actors and you need
examples from all genres to show to prospective
employers."

Phillip Mittel
Motion Artists Agency

Getting a Gig

9

When I first arrived in Los Angeles I knew a total of three people who worked in the industry. I called each one of them and reminded them that they were, in part, responsible for my making the move. I was fortunate. Work came only two days later, constructing props and painting sets for a special effects company. I had made it clear that I was willing to do *anything*.

For the next two years I took everything that came my way in terms of work. I scattered beef brains at 3 a.m. on a butcher's set floor. Shoveled cow poop in a pasture to clear a picnic set. Drove 80 mph in a rainstorm to replace a neon fixture in a bar location. I worked on films with scripts that included scenes I would never want to see in the theater. It was all bankable experience. I said yes to everything and learned skills on the fly. Whenever I was asked if I could do something that I didn't really know how to do I tried to flash a confident smile and then went about learning how to do it, if not brilliantly, at least competently.

Most of my work came through word of mouth. If a gig went well, I tried to stay in touch with my coworkers and made sure they knew how to reach me if and when another project came along. In addition, I expanded my storyboard portfolio by working with young directors just finishing school or breaking into the business. This means that I found myself on very low-budget and even no-budget projects, but I was able to forge new relationships and create boards that were based on real-world experiences rather than theoretic exercises.

In Los Angeles there are numerous film schools and university departments that are constantly churning out graduates in directing and cinematography. These filmmakers often need assistance in visualizing their projects. There are fewer storyboard artists than directing novices. I printed up a flyer with examples of my work and a contact number and posted them at the American Film Institute and UCLA. Within a few weeks I had formed relationships with two directors and was storyboarding their films. With that expanded portfolio, I then went around introducing myself to a series of production houses.

Strategy

First you need to identify those businesses in your area that might have a need for storyboards or other types of pre-visualization documents. Make a list of:

- Film schools
- Universities that have departments of film, communication, or drama
- Video production houses — especially those that produce music videos
- Advertising agencies
- CD-ROM and DVD development companies
- Web site designers who use motion graphics

Internships

The above list can all be excellent places to start introducing yourself. If you can afford to work as an intern for a short while, then draft a proposal that will show best what you have to offer. Often these internships turn into paid work if you can demonstrate to the company that you can meet deadlines and improve their work environment. One word of warning though: If you accept an internship position, be very clear as to the parameters of what you are willing to offer in terms of time. Two months is reasonable, two years is not. Make this clear up front so there will be no misunderstanding when you are ready to move on (or up).

Flat-fee Arrangement

Another situation that you may be offered early in your career is the flat-fee arrangement. In this setup you will be paid a fixed amount to do the job (i.e., a 20-minute dramatic script being produced for the film festival circuit). This can often be a great way to meet people with more experience and good connections to future work. However, the flip side is that you are trading your work on a script for a set, usually limited, amount of money. If there are extensive changes to the script or other revisions, you may find yourself working ad infinitum on what you thought was going to be a 10-day gig.

That was my position on my first paid job. For room, board, and a small flat fee, I agreed to storyboard an entire feature. I later calculated that I had been paid less than the rental on one of the klieg lights. I do not regret a moment. It was trial by fire (or ice, in that chilly Cape Cod autumn) and I happily showed up on the set each day to draw, move furniture, or do whatever else that might cross the production designer's mind that day. When I signed my contract though, I somehow had enough sense to have a clause that included an ending date. In other words, I said yes to the flat fee, but only until the tenth of December, which was the estimated last day of shooting. And, as often happens, shooting went over the expected finish day. From that day on, if they wanted a storyboard artist on the set, they needed to pay an additional fee. Was it much money? Of course not. Did it keep the relationship clean between the producers and me? Absolutely, because no one needed to ask a favor.

Sliding Scale

Once I reached a state in my working life where I felt I could pick and choose a bit, I realized that there was an inverse relationship between content and money. In other words, for a commercial that had basically no content aside from the product it was seeking to advertise, I was offered a high fee. On the other hand, the small, independent features that I yearned to be involved with often didn't have very much money for preproduction expenses. My solution was to institute a sliding scale for my services that ensured the ad agencies and TV studios paid top prices while independent films and small music videos were charged a reduced rate.

This approach is not for everyone, and if you are working through an agent, he or she may not like this arrangement at all. But for me it was a solution to my own desire to stay available for small, edgy projects that couldn't necessarily afford my going fees.

Agencies

Once your career is underway and you have a solid portfolio of work to present, you might want to consider finding an agent. There are a number of issues involved with this type of representation.

Do you want to be on call every day, all day? Many agents require that you carry a beeper and be available at a call's notice. If you are a fast-track person, this will suit your pace; but if you want to carve out a part-time niche for yourself, it may not be a good fit.

There are many reasons to have an agent. Your agent can act as a go-between in your contract negotiations. This can often lead to higher day rates and better fringe benefits, such as the use of a car on location or overtime pay. They will be responsible for paying you rather than the production house or ad agency. This can alleviate the headache of tardy payments for work done months before.

Another reason to use an agent is for their depth of connections within the industry. It's their job to have information regarding all the current and future productions in your area.

"What I look for in a portfolio is diversity. If you only want to do film, then the supply and demand will make it more difficult to work all the time. I need to see how tight an artist can work. I get calls for loose drawings from some production houses, but in order to send an artist every day, I need him to be able to work on many levels of polish. You need to look at the best artists out there and try to come up to their standards. We have lots of artists that come from a background in comic book art as well as classically trained illustrators. We also look for a solid understanding of film language."

Mark Miller
founder of Famous Frames, an agency that handles storyboard artists and illustrators

"If you have a portfolio of westerns, they probably won't hire you for a sci-fi film. Also, it helps to have work using a variety of media such as pencil, marker and computer. I look for great skills in drawing as well as a sharp sense of designing the frame. Many of our artists trained as transportation designers before transferring into entertainment design. Now they do it all: theme parks, creatures, and special effects as well as traditional film."

Phillip Mittel
founder of Motion Artists, an agency that places artists, production designers, concept artists, and digital designers

While you are busy working on a show, they will be looking out for your next gig. Some agents will even work as career managers, counseling you on which productions will add the most interest to your portfolio or setting up meetings with hot new directors who may be getting their first features in the coming months.

An agency will typically take a 25% cut out of the artist's fee, although that can be reduced over time if the artist stays with the agency and works regularly. Even with this cut, agencies can often negotiate higher fees, so the artist can find more in his or her pocket in the end. Some agencies ask for an exclusive contract, while others will allow outside work. These points are usually decided on a case-by-case basis. If you have many good contacts within your industry, an agent may not be able to offer you enough to make the relationship worthwhile. But if you are an artist who would rather not spend time with the details of business, then an agent may be the way to go.

If you're not sure whether going through an agency is right for you, ask yourself a few questions:

Does the agency require that all the work you book be funneled through them and that they get a piece of it, even if the job came through your own connections?

How quickly will they pay you for your work? Some agencies work on a 30-day net, some take even longer to get you your wages. On the other hand, if you are hired directly by a production company, the checks are usually cut on a weekly or bi-weekly schedule.

Do you want the security of the agency dealing directly with the production company? You are then saved from having to make your own contracts and the worry of — if the company is unknown to you — whether it will honor its commitments.

Do you like being part of a team and having someone else closely involved with the path of your career? If so, then an agent might fit well into your plan. If you are by nature a loner and value autonomy, then you might want to stay independent and make your own connections.

Unions

The union for illustrators and matte artists is IATSE (International Alliance of Theater and Employees) Local #790. They were founded in 1945, at the end of the war, when many returning servicemen were looking for employment in the booming film industry. As of publication, there are currently 156 members, and about 85 are employed on union productions.

If you are working under a union contract, you are assured of receiving health insurance, pension, and other benefits rarely offered to freelancers or artists working as independent contractors. Because most storyboard work these days is available on a freelance basis (as of the end of the studio era), many artists want to work as a part of a group that sets wage minimums, working conditions, and offers some of the options, like health coverage, that freelance workers often lack.

The Catch (22, that is...)

In order to join the union, you need to have worked 30 days on a union production. In order to work on a union production, you usually need to be in the union. Aye, there's the rub. This strange set of circumstances can be overcome in a few different ways. First, once all the members on the union roster are working, a production may hire anyone they wish to fill the position of illustrator or storyboard artist. This situation is rare, but occasionally the roster has 100% employment of eligible artists, and non-union workers may be hired onto a union signatory production.

You can also gain entrance by working a non-union film that becomes union. All your hours, even those worked before the union contract, become union hours, and if you've got thirty days at the end of production, you will be "grandfathered" onto the roster.

There is a new way to become a member, which is to work 30 days on a signatory of AICP, the Alliance of Commercial Producers. Once you have those days, you can register with an organization called Contract Services, which keeps records of your days worked, and after another 90 days on a signatory production you will be admitted to 790.

The cost of joining the union is based on the current base salary of a senior illustrator: $374.73 per day (as of publication). You may also join the union as a junior, which has a base rate of $332.46. The admittance dues are equal to two weeks senior gross pay, or $3302.18, 50% due on completing your application and the rest due at the initiation. In addition, there are also yearly dues, currently running $206.85 per quarter.

Local 790 of IATSE is a useful resource for artists who live and work in areas where IATSE is active. Aside from the media centers of Los Angeles and New York, it will probably not be necessary to join in order to obtain a position on a crew.

Freelance or Team Player?

From the time I graduated college until I took my first position as a teacher, I worked as a freelance designer and illustrator for 14 years. Every few months I changed jobs, met new coworkers, and explored challenges of designing for theater and film that I could not have imagined existed before I was faced with solving them. Under these conditions I thrived. It's not for everyone. Here's a quick checklist:

Roller coasters	Row boats
Hotel rooms	Home-cooked meals
Surprise parties	Casual Fridays
Spontaneity	Long-range planning
Shifting deadlines	Staying on schedule

If the items on the left annoy or frustrate you, consider looking for in-house employment. If you can't get enough of those loop-de-loops and can laugh at the shifting sands, then you might have a freelance temperament.

Summary

In the end, how you structure your entry into the art and business of preproduction visualization should be based on individual needs. Is there a medium that you are attracted to more than the rest? How much do you want to work, and do you want to travel for extended periods of time? Do you have an independent character or do you like being one of an ongoing team? All these issues can inform the path you take once your career is underway. Until then, take what comes and keep your eyes open for any opportunity that might cross your path.

Signing Off...

This journey has taken us through the world of representation and abstraction, imagery and the written word in an effort to guide and assist you in communicating your inner vision. Whether you keep your pre-viz documents to yourself or publish them for all the world to see, I hope that the ideas and the tools in these chapters will aid you in your creative process. The making of a film, video, or CD-ROM can be an expansive challenge. Let yourself play with new ways of seeing and your stories will take on new forms of expression.

Thanks for your time and attention.

Appendix I:

DVD List of Titles with Storyboards and Other Preproduction Visualization Documents

DVD List of Titles with Storyboards and Other Preproduction Visualization Documents

1) **Do The Right Thing** (Criterion)
   Director: Spike Lee
   Original storyboards for the riot sequence, plus a film-to-storyboard comparison

2) **The Rock** (Criterion)
   Director: Michael Bay
   Storyboards
   Production design drawings

3) **12 Monkeys** (Universal Studios)
   Director: Terry Gilliam
   Storyboards and production stills

4) **Spartacus** (Criterion)
   Director: Stanley Kubrick
   Original storyboards by Saul Bass
   Hundreds of production stills, lobby cards, posters, print ads, and a comic book
   Sketched by director Stanley Kubrick

5) **Rififi** (Criterion)
   Director: Jules Dassin
   Production design drawings and stills

6) **The Red Shoes** (Criterion)
   Director: Michael Powell
   The Red Shoes Sketches: animated film of Heinrich Heckroth's painted storyboards, with a comparison to "The Red Shoes" ballet

7) **Silence of the Lambs** (Criterion)
   Director: Jonathon Demme
   Film-to-storyboard comparison & storyboards

8) **The 39 Steps** (Criterion)
   Director: Alfred Hitchcock
   Original production design drawings

9) **Dead Ringers** (Criterion)
   Director: David Cronenberg
   The original designs for the opening credit sequence
   Drawings and photographs of the medical instruments and
   sculptures designed for the movie

10) **Seven** (New Line Platinum Series)
    Director: David Fincher
    Animated storyboards
    Production design

11) **Dark City** (New Line Platinum Series)
    Director: Alex Proyas
    Set designs

12) **Blade** (New Line Platinum Series)
    Director: Stephen Norrington
    Pencil sketches through production designs

13) **Jurassic Park & Lost World: Limited Collectors Edition Box
    Set – 1999** (Universal Studios)
    Director: Steven Spielberg
    Jurassic Park includes: documentary, preproduction meetings,
    storyboards, foley artists, Phil Tippett animatics, production
    photos and notes.
    Lost World includes: documentary, deleted scenes, illustrations
    and conceptual drawings and storyboards, models, *The World of
    Jurassic Park*

14) ***Fight Club*** (CBS/FOX Home Video)
Director: David Fincher
Still Galleries: set design stills, costume stills, original sketches,
oil paintings, storyboards, publicity stills, lobby cards &
production stills

15) ***The Perfect Storm*** (Warner Home Video)
Director: Wolfgang Petersen
Storyboard Gallery

16) ***The Nutty Professor II – The Klumps (Collectors Edition)***
(Universal Studios)
Director: Peter Segal
Storyboards

17) ***Rushmore – Collector's Edition*** (Criterion Collection)
Director: Wes Anderson
Wes Anderson's hand-drawn storyboards, plus a film-to-
storyboard comparison

18) ***The Wizard of Oz*** (Warner Home Video)
Director: Victor Fleming
Portrait gallery, special effects stills, and stills from the Hollywood
premiere, original sketches and storyboards, costume designs
and make-up tests

19) ***Jaws (25th Anniversary Widescreen Collector's Edition)***
DTS (Universal/MCA)
Director: Steven Spielberg
Jaws Archives: Photos, storyboards, and production drawings

20) ***Men in Black (Collector's Series)*** – DTS (Columbia/TriStar)
Director: Barry Sonnenfeld
Storyboard comparisons, conceptual art gallery, production
photo gallery

21) **The Abyss – Special Edition** (20th Century Fox)
    Director: James Cameron
    Comprehensive film analysis from storyboards and concept art
    to final release

22) **Brazil** (Criterion Collection)
    Director: Terry Gilliam
    "The Production Notebook," screenwriters Tom Stoppard and
    Charles McKeown illuminate the script's development through 3
    drafts and 3 treatments. Production designer Norman Garwood
    displays his designs for *Brazil*'s unique sets. Costume designer
    James Acheson explores the couture of fashion, fantasy, and
    fascism. Terry Gilliam's original dream sequences, in
    storyboards, include hundreds of shots that never made it to
    the screen. Composer Michael Kamen unveils the sources of his
    score. A study of the special effects includes footage of unused
    effects

23) **Robocop** (Criterion Collection)
    Director: Paul Verhoeven
    Film-to-storyboard comparison
    Storyboards

24) **The Cell** (New Line Platinum Series)
    Director: Tarsem
    Examination of the film's special effects, production design,
    make-up and costumes

25) **Pleasantville** (New Line Platinum Series)
    Director: Gary Ross
    Storyboard gallery

26) **Spawn** (New Line Platinum Series)
    Director: Mark ZA Dippe
    Scene-to-storyboard comparisons
    Original Todd McFarlane sketches

27) **Vertigo** – Collector's Edition (Universal)
Director: Alfred Hitchcock
Storyboards, Production drawings, production photographs and
advertising materials

28) **The Birds** (Universal)
Director: Alfred Hitchcock
Storyboard Sequence & Newsreel

29) **The 39 Steps** (Criterion Collection)
Director: Alfred Hitchcock
Original production design drawings

30) **American Beauty – The Awards Edition**
(Dreamworks/Universal)
Director: Sam Mendes
Exclusive Storyboards with commentary by director Mendes and
Director of Photography Conrad Hall

31) **Independence Day – Special Edition** (20th Century Fox)
Director: Roland Emmerich
Production stills gallery, storyboards gallery & concept art
gallery

32) **Terminator 2 - Judgement Day – The Ultimate DVD Edition**
(Artisan Entertainment)
Director: James Cameron
Over 700 Storyboards

33) **The Sixth Sense** (Buena Vista Home Entertainment)
Director: M. Night Shyamalan
Storyboard to film comparisons

34) **The Nightmare Before Christmas – Special Edition**
(Buena Vista Home Entertainment)
Director: Henry Selick
Gallery of concept art, character design and animation tests
Deleted footage – animated sequences and storyboards not
used in the final film

35) ***The City of Lost Children*** (Columbia/TriStar Home Video)
Director: Jean-Pierre Jeunet, Marc Caro
Costume design gallery
Production sketch gallery

36) ***Taxi Driver: Special Edition*** (Columbia/TriStar Home Video)
Director: Martin Scorsese
Photo montage/portrait gallery, storyboard sequence &
advertising materials

37) ***Dogma – Special Edition*** (Columbia/TriStar Home Video)
Director: Kevin Smith
Complete set of storyboards from three major scenes

Appendix II:

Computer Applications with Pre-visualization Capabilities

Computer Applications with Pre-visualization Capabilities

The following titles are consumer-level versions of imaging software. There are many high-end applications as well, but this list will focus on software that is appropriate for storyboarding and other pre-visualization uses.

INSPIRATION

Use: Non-linear brainstorming (and other visual thinking tasks)

Inspiration is a program that is intuitive to use and fast to learn. It provides the user with easy-to-manipulate templates that can be arranged in patterns of your choice. Each idea "bubble" can contain text or images and also can be expressed with different forms and colors. It supports visual thinking in the concept stage and beyond. The program is supported by a wonderful **Web site** (www.inspiration.com) and is also available in a children's version. Highly recommended for planning, concept development, flowcharts, non-linear thinking, and thumbnail sketch frames.

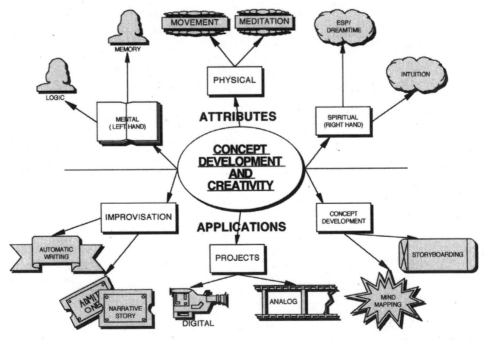

Concept diagram developed using Inspiration

BRYCE 4

Use: A 3-D application that allows you to create sets and exterior locations, and then send a camera through them recording a QT movie.

Bryce 4 has a little bit of everything. Although it can render remarkable exterior locations and very detailed architecture, it can also be used to build simple 3-D sets that can be used for shot planning. If you are planning to be on a set or location for a number of days, it may be worth the time to build a small digital set and play around with the camera provided. You can make Quicktime movies or pop off snap shots to use in a 2-D storyboard. And if you feel like exploring further, the software comes complete with a library full of textures, objects, skies, and terrain that can transport you to another world. The learning curve is moderate but the intuitive interface makes it a fun activity. The program is not that useful for quick sketch purposes.

Web site: www3.corel.com

Storyboard for *The Fifth Element* using Bryce 4

PHOTOSHOP

Use: Photo manipulation

A popular software package, *Photoshop* is the industry standard for photo manipulation. Scan printed images or load directly from digital sources and you can shift contrast, de-saturate colors, or tweak an unruly tuft of hair. Scan in location photos and the drawing tools will let you add your own figure sketches or import figures from *Poser* and collage a photo storyboard for presentations.

Web site:
www.adobe.com/products/
photoshop/main.html

POSER

Use: A digital model to pose and use as reference. Also can be output and pasted into storyboard.

Poser has an easy interface that allows you, with a bit of practice, to arrange the provided figures into any position. You can then change the 'camera's' POV and render a figure to paste onto your storyboard or simply work in wire-frame mode and use the model as reference. You can also use one of dozens of preset *Poser* figures, select from the provided clothing and get results in a shorter amount of time. The software has many high end uses, but is priced for the casual user to enjoy as well.

Web site:
www.curiouslabs.com

Student storyboard by Timothy Kendall using Photoshop and Poser

STORYBOARD ARTIST and STORYBOARD QUICK

Uses: Simple storyboards for film and television

Storyboard Artist and *Storyboard Quick* offer the user a dedicated 2-D clip-file of imagery that can be layered together to form storyboard frames. The programs come complete with backgrounds, figures, and props that can be arranged in aspect ratios ranging from TV to wide-screen formats. You can also print out the frames in a variety of patterns, from a single drawing per page to 16 thumbnails per sheet. Although limited in scope by the simplicity of the drawings provided, these programs offer an alternative to sketching your own images.

Web site: www.powerproduction.com

 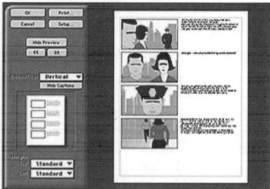

Screen shots from Storyboard Artist

A few more software applications to mention:

SCRIPTWERX
Uses: A formatting software that works with Microsoft Word to create film scripts. Has a storyboard function that aligns the boards to the script pages
Web site: www.ScriptWerx.com

ADOBE PREMIERE
Uses: An editing program that allows you to import storyboard frames and play them back with timed transitions and soundtrack.
Web site: www.adobe.com

BOARDMASTER
Uses: Animatics, an in-motion version of storyboarding. Gives the user the ability to build images in various aspect ratios, transition between images, and time the playback for an in-action board presentation.
Web site: www.boardmastersoftware.com

SHOTMASTER
Uses: *ShotMaster* does two main jobs. First, it provides a place to keep notes relative to any scene. Second, it helps you create a shot list with simple, self-drawn diagrams, drag-and-drop storyboards, or scans of hand-drawn storyboards. These shot lists then can be printed in an easy-to-read form, complete with thumbnail versions of the storyboards and shot diagrams.
Web site: www.badhamcompany.com

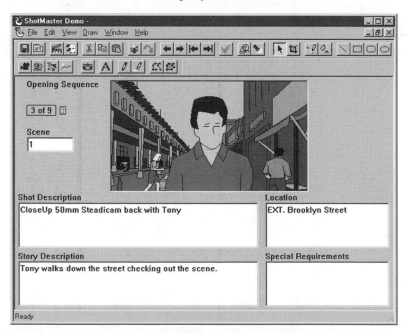

Screen shot from Shotmaster

Appendix III:

Internet Film and Video Sites with Visualization Content

Internet Film and Video Sites with Visualization Content

DIRECTORS

The Directors Guild of America
http://www.dga.org

STANLEY KUBRICK

Stanley Kubrick: The Master Filmmaker
Biography, filmography, and more
http://pages.prodigy.com/kubrick

The Authorized Stanley Kubrick Web Site
Warner Bros. creates the second official Kubrick-related site.
http://www.kubrickfilms.com

Kubrick MultiMedia Film Guide
http://www.indelibleinc.com/kubrick/
Images and sounds from Kubrick's works including *Clockwork Orange*, *2001*, and *Dr. Strangelove*

The Kubrick Site Mirror
The Kubrick Site is the official Web resource of the alt.movies.kubrick newsgroup; it has been established as a non-profit resource archive for documentary materials regarding, in whole or in part, the work of the late American film director.
http://www.visual-memory.co.uk/amk

Other Stanley Kubrick Links
http://www.geocities.com/SunsetStrip/Studio/5139/kubrick.html

ALFRED HITCHCOCK

Alfred Hitchcock – The Master of Suspense
The site contains a biography, filmography, essay and more.
http://nextdch.mty.itesm.mx/~plopezg/Kaplan/Hitchcock.html

The Hitchcock Page
This site includes a shot by shot look at the famous shower sequence from *Psycho*.
http://www.primenet.com/~mwc

Psycho
This site is devoted solely to Hitchcock's 1960 masterpiece.
http://www.geocities.com/Hollywood/1645

Hitchcock Online
http://www.qumulus.nl/hitchcock

The 'MacGuffin' Web Page
Alfred Hitchcock scholars meet here!
http://www.labyrinth.net.au/~muffin

JEAN-LUC GODARD

Cinema = Jean-Luc Godard
An extensive collection of essays and links on the Freanch New Wave's Most profilic and iconoclastic director
http://www.geocities.com/Hollywood/Cinema/4355

To, For and Against: Jean-Luc Godard
http://user.chollian.net/~ml2000

Jean Luc Godard – The official website
http://ixvm.com/godard

AKIRA KUROSAWA

Tribute to Akiro Kurosawa
http://www.1worldfilms.com/Tribute%20Akira%20Kurosawa.htm

Akira Kurosawa Filmography + Biography
http://www2.tky.3web.ne.jp/~adk/kurosawa/AKpage.html

Kurosawa Akira: A Teacher of Courage
From Japan Echo
http://www.japanecho.co.jp/docs/html/250614.html

Tod Browning – Director of *Dracula* (1931) and *Freaks* (1932)
Includes bio and links to related sites.
http://search.yahoo.com/search?p=film+Related+sites

Paul Thomas Anderson: Cigarettes & Coffee
Definitive site for P.T.A.'s (*Hard Eight*, *Boogie Nights*, *Magnolia*) budding career as one of the American "New Wave" film writer/directors
http://www.ptanderson.com/home.htm

AFI OnLine Presents Robert Wise: American Filmmaker
http://www.afionline.org/wise/robert_wise.html

CINEMATOGRAPHY + CINEMATOGRAPHERS

Cinematography World
Provides news and information on the art, technology, and business of cinematography.
http://www.cinematographyworld.com

American Cinematographer
http://www.cinematographer.com/magazine

American Society of Cinematographers
http://www.cinematographer.com

Gregg Toland
Orson Welles's *Citizen Kane* and Cinematography
http://www.pathfinder.com/photo/essay/kane/kane.htm

The Society of Operating Cameramen
http://www.soc.org

The History of Cinematography
Comprehensive site on the development of the moving image
http://www.precinemahistory.net

Steven Bradford's Electronic Cinematography
Topics include NTSC video signal, D/Vision editing
http://www.seanet.com/~bradford

Nibley, Christopher S.
Live action, visual effects, blue screen and motion control cinematography
http://www.nibley.com

STORYBOARDING/ PRODUCTION DESIGN

Brazil Storyboards, etc.
Excellent resource for exploring the controversies and difficulties that surrounded the making of the lauded motion picture
http://www.trond.com/brazil

TRON Storyboards
Revised drafts of the script for *Tron* were accompanied by detailed storyboard sketches. These storyboards would prove to be invaluable.
http://www.3gcs.com/tron/ production/Storyboards

Twister Storyboards
http://www.movies.warnerbros.com/ twister/cmp/storyboards.html

Troops Storyboards
Here is a collection of storyboards used in *Troops.*
http://www.theforce.net/troops/ t_story.shtml

Dan's Unoffical Wing Commander Movie Website
Storyboards of *Wing Commander*
http://www.users.nac.net/splat/wc/ images_storyboards.htm

South Park Storyboards
Official South Park site on Comedy Central
http://www.comcentral.com/ southpark/storyboards/story10.shtml

Star Wars: Dewback Storyboards
http://www.starwars.com/dewback/ three/noframes/storyboard1.html

Deep Blue Sea Storyboards
http://www.deepbluesea.net/cmp/ storyboardslq.html

The Big Lebowski
The making of a Coen Brothers film
http://members.aol.com/WPRob/ lebowskibook.html

The Making of Enemy of the State
http://www.atnzone.com/ enemyofthestate.shtml

The Making Of Hollywood's Hit Movies
Insider secrets, photos, history, storyboards, video interviews, clips from the movies
http://www.themakingof.com

Pretty as a Picture: The Art of David Lynch
80 minute documentary about the director and the making of the film *Lost Highway*
http://www.finecut.com

Dune: Behind The Scenes
About the making of David Lynch's film
http://www.flg21.com/dune

Bride Of Frankenstein (1935)
Description and history of the making of the film
http://www.filmsite.org/bride.html

Storyboarding

What is a Storyboard? History of Storyboards, the Purpose of a Storyboard, How to Make a Storyboard, Storyboards for Multimedia Presentations, etc.
http://w3.tvi.cc.nm.us/~jvelez/MMS170/storyboard

Alexandre Trauner: 50 Years of Cinema

Set designer for the likes of Welles, Wilder, Huston
http://www.lpce.com/trauner

The Set Decorators' Society of America

http://www.setdecorators.org

LA - 411

The bible of any L.A.-based filmmaker looking for contacts in all fields of making films. Great for sets, costumes, props, expendables etc.
http://la411.com

VISUAL EFFECTS

The Matrix

http://www.whatisthematrix.com

Cinefex

The online guide to the ultimate in visual effects
http://www.cinefex.com

The Reel Site

Movie reviews, movie news, movie forums & more
Learn about special effects by reading interviews and articles.
Special emphasis on Industrial Light + Magic.
http://www.thereelsite.com

Visual FX.com

http://www.visualfx.com

CineSecrets

Insights and technical information about the making of *Star Wars* and other films
http://www.CineSecrets.com

Infinite 3D Effects Computer Animation

Computer animation, 3D animation, digital effects, 3D modeling, photo-real
http://www.infinite3dfx.com/links.html

Industrial Video, Film TV

Animation, compositing, 3D surfacing, Visual Effects Society
http://www.visual-effects-society.org

Visual Magic Magazine

http://visualmagic.awn.com

Gnomon Inc.

School of 3D Visual Effects
http://www.gnomon3d.com

Talk like the Animals - A look at Dr. Dolittle's Visual Effects

http://www.cinematographer.com/magazine/dec98/Animals

Thinking Small

A look at *Small Soldiers'* visual effects
http://www.cinematographer.com/magazine/dec98/Soldiers

Tearing Up the Town

A look at *Godzilla's* visual effects
http://www.cinematographer.com/magazine/dec98/Town

The Visual Effects Resource Center

Current Visual Effects news and information
http://www.visualfx.com

The Making of Darth Vader's Mask
http://www.ketzer.com/
DV_lifesized.html

HomeGrafica Obscura
A compilation of technical notes, pictures, essays for computer graphics
http://www.sgi.com/grafica

Rhythm & Hues Studios
Produces animation and special effects for movies, commercials, television
http://www.rhythm.com

Alias/Wavefront
Developer of software for digital media content creation
http://www.aliaswavefront.com

HomeDark Horizons
Latest news on films in production (mainly dealing with blockbuster, sci-fi, and fantasy films). A good insightful site with fan reviews and QuickTime trailers of up and coming films.
http://www.darkhorizons.com/
news.htm

SGI
Designs and supplies a family of interactive 3-D graphics and digital media technologies
http://www.sgi.com

Pacific Data Images
Computer graphics for film and video whose credits include *Batman Forever*
http://www.pdi.com

MISC. FILM REFERENCE SITES

Internet Movie Database (IMDB)
Great site for actor, director, writer, producer biographies and timeline. Very basic but concise information for whomever one chooses to search for.
http://imdb.com

Women In Film Homepage
http://www.wif.org

America Cinema Editors
http://www.ace-filmeditors.org

Society of Motion Picture and Television Art Directors
http://www.artdirectors.org

Academy of Motion Picture Arts and Sciences
Official site for the professional organization with a special section on the annual Academy Awards
http://www.oscars.org

The Official Academy Awards Site
http://www.oscars.com

American Movie Classics (AMC)
http://www.amctv.com

Classic Films
Includes hundreds of images, original articles on film and film making, bibliography, audio clips. A must-see for classic film fans.
http://www.moderntimes.com/palace

Britmovie
Dedicated to classic British films, cinema and movies
http://www.britmovie.co.uk

The Silents Majority
The home page of The Silents Majority Classic Film Fan Club, the source for information on silent film on the Internet
http://www.mdle.com/ClassicFilms

The Greatest Films
The greatest films in cinematic history: greatest moments, famous scenes, and film quotes. Organized by historical decades, years, and genres.
http://www.filmsite.org
http://www.greatestfilms.org

The Big List of Movie Mistakes
Large collection of continuity mistakes and film trivia.
http://www.movie-mistakes.com

Criterion Collection
Continuing series of classic & contemporary films on laserdisc and DVD. Features clips, art, and essays on every film in the collection.
http://www.criterionco.com

Hershey Theatre – Classic Films
The Classic Film Series was designed to recreate movie-going of the 1940s, 50s.
http://www.hersheytheatre.com

Dreams: the Terry Gilliam Fanzine
http://www.smart.co.uk/dreams

Big movies
Cinema site for small movies
http://www.city-net.com/~fodder/info/about.html

Kodak
http://www.kodak.com/US/en/motion

Wide Angle/Closeup
Interviews, behind-the-scenes production stories, and photo essays, featuring some of today's leading film artists and craftspeople
http://members.aol.com/morgands1/closeup/indices/mainmenu.htm

Large Format Cinema Association
http://www.lfca.org

Martin Hart's American WideScreen Museum
http://www.simplecom.net/widefilm

American Film Institute (AFI)
National arts organization dedicated to preserving the heritage of film and television
http://www.afionline.org

The American Museum of the Moving Image
Dedicated to educating the public about the art, history, technique, and technology of film, television, and digital media, and to examining their impact on culture and society
http://www.ammi.org/site/site.asp

The British Film Institute (BFI)
The BFI is the UK's national body for film, television, and the moving image, comprising collections and archives, cinema exhibition and education.
www.bfi.org.uk/

Making Scenes
Ottawa's Lesbian & Gay Film & Video Festival
http://Fox.nstn.ca/~scenes

Fan Sites
The Internet's Largest Film & Media directory with links to over 20,000 global sites
http://www.afionline.org/cinemedia/welcomes/you.html

The History of Cinematography
Comprehensive site on the development of the moving image
http://www.precinemahistory.net

Foreignfilms
Fantastic site for the foreign film fanatic allows one to choose film, country, and/or director.
http://www.foreignfilms.com

Hometown Cinema
Dedicated to student films and filmmakers. The site has a screening room in which you can submit your own films over the Internet or simply watch other student films.
http://hometown.z.com/home.html

Film Underground
A tips and tricks site for digital filmmakers
http://www.filmunderground.com

Cyberfilmschool
Another tips and tricks site for digital filmmakers (with lots of links).
http://www.cyberfilmschool.com

filmfilm.com
A pitching site for films and internet shorts. Contains a screening room and prizes.
http://www.filmfilm.com

LittleGoldenGuy.com
A nice reference site dedicated to all Oscar winners from 1927 to current
http://www.littlegoldenguy.com

Scriptsales.com
A site devoted to script pitches and sales
http://www.scriptsales.com

NYScreenwriter
A site based on the NYScreenwriter magazine (loads of competitions for writers).
http://www.nyscreenwriter.com

Thrae.com
Explores "micro-budget" films and no-budget solutions to filmmakers' problems.
http://www.thrae.com

Script-O-Rama
The ultimate site to find various drafts of screenplays in their entirety
http://www.script-o-rama.com

The Movie Times
Detailed site reviewing box office tallies from past to current.
http://www.the-movie-times.com

INTERNET VIDEO BROADCASTERS/ FILMMAKING LINKS
(subject to dot-com disappearance)

The iFilm Network
Committed to broadening the scope, enhancing the quality, and widening the availability of films and filmed entertainment for a mass audience
http://www.ifilm.net

AtomShockwave.com
Find, play, create, and share shocked
entertainment, from cartoons and comics
to music and games. Plus a large collection of films and shorts
http://www.shockwave.com
http://www.atomfilms.com

IPIX
Visual content solutions for the Internet
http://www.ipix.com

CinemaNow.com
Digital studio/theater venue lets you
watch, make, win, buy, or talk about
movies.
http://www.cinemanow.com

Independent Feature Project West
Provides information and support for the
independent film community and spon-
sors the annual Spirit Awards.
http://www.ifpwest.org

Davenport Films
Recreates traditional folk and fairy tales
in American settings.
http://www.oz.net/~davfilms

Making Film
Focuses on independent filmmaking by
providing news, reviews, festival information, and more.
http://www.ifmagazine.com

**The Winnipeg Film Group &
Cinematheque**
A filmmaking resource for funding
http://www.winnipegfilmgroup.mb.ca

Filmmaking.Free
35mm filmmaking hands-on training in
France.
http://filmmaking.free.fr

DV Filmmaker
Provides articles, interviews, tips, links,
and other resources for those making a
DV feature film.
http://www.dvfilmmaker.com

NOVA: Avalanche!
The art of filmmaking meets the science
of natural disasters
http://www.pbs.org/wgbh/nova/
avalanche

Small Movies
Focuses on the equipment, methods,
techniques, and general craft of making
cinema.
http://www.city-net.com/~fodder

**Short Attention Span Film and
Video Festival**
Festival for short works in all formats
http://www.sasfvf.com

IndieWire
A high-end mag, attuned to American
indies especially, great with news from
festivals, etc.
http://indiewire.com

24 Frames Per Second
Online film journal with its very own
"best films of all time" section
http://www.24framespersecond.com

cine16
Research and cinema site for 16mm educational, anthropological, documentary, animated, and art films. Ongoing film festival.
http://www.cine16.com

Videomaker
Online version of monthly magazine covers the use of camcorders, desktop video, editing, lighting, and audio production for novice and expert videographers alike.
http://www.videomaker.com/scripts/index.cfm

FilmmakerStore
Has industry standard software for screenwriters, storyboard artists, and filmmakers.
http://www.scriptwerx.com

CineWEB
Film & video making community, providing lists of properties suitable for filming, contacts for completing production, and more
http://www.cineweb.com

CineWEB's Connections
A place where you can find just about anything that has anything to do with the film and video industry
http://www.cineweb.com/connections

movies.net
Production resources development, Cyber Film School, has various templates and forms for budgets, proposals, and storyboards.
http://www.movies.net/production.html

FilmMaker
Articles, links, files, and other resources for filmmakers
http://www.filmmaker.com

The Sundance Institute
http://www.sundance.org

Mediatrip
Nice multimedia site that allows one to view and vote on favorite shorts, film and video releases.
http://www.mediatrip.com

4 Filmmakers
An extensive site that that covers what is currently in development and has a screenwriters submission form open to critics
http://4filmmakers.com

Editors Net
A technical page that covers interviews with current editors and their equipment
http://www.editorsnet.com

CINEMA STUDIES

To Kill a Mockingbird: Scripts and Storyboards
English On-Line is a New Zealand site for English teachers with fully resourced teaching units, links to sites, an Internet tutorial, projects for students, and a discussion forum.
http://www.english.unitecnology.ac.nz/resources/units/mockingbird/scripts.html

P.O.V. Interactive
Online companion to Point Of View, a PBS series airing independent documentaries
http://www.pbs.org/pov

Society of Cinema Studies
http://www.cinemastudies.org

Society for Cinema Studies: Archival News
This new column is designed to be a regular feature of Cinema Journal.
http://www.cinemastudies.org/allcolumns.htm

Motion Picture and Television Reading Room (Library of Congress)
http://lcweb.loc.gov/rr/mopic

Motion Pictures in the Library of Congress
http://lcweb.loc.gov/rr/mopic/mpcoll.html

International Historic Films, Inc.
Military, political, and social history of the 20th century on videocassette. Newsreels, documentaries, feature films, nazi and Soviet propaganda. Classic American, British, and Russian films.
http://www.IHFfilm.com

Quest Pictures
Film students and recent graduates dedicated to making the 16mm feature
http://www.questpictures.com

Instrumental Productions
Making home movies for fun and entertainment.
http://www.instruments.org

Museum of Modern Art New York
http://www.moma.org

STUDIO SITES

20th Century Fox
http://www.foxmovies.com

Fox Searchlight
http://www.foxsearchlight.com

Columbia/TriStar
http://www.sony.com/goto-movies

Sony Pictures Classics
http://spe.sony.com/classics

Disney
http://www.disneypictures.com

DreamWorks SKG
http://www.dreamworks.com

Miramax
http://www.miramax.com

New Line
http://www.newline.com

Fine Line
http://www.flf.com

Paramount
http://www.paramount.com

Paramount Classics
http://www.paramountclassics.com

Universal
http://www.unistudios.com

Warner Bros.
http://www2.warnerbros.com

Artisan Entertainment
http://www.artisanent.com

Castle Rock Entertainment
http://castle-rock.com

Lions Gate Entertainment
http://www.lionsgate-ent.com

New Regency Productions
http://www.newregency.com

October Films
http://www.octoberfilms.com

FILM INDUSTRY SITES

Variety
Industry trade magazine gives you daily articles of films in preproduction, production, & post production.
Note: Must subscribe to get full stories.
http://www.variety.com

The Hollywood Reporter
Industry trade magazine gives you daily articles of films in preproduction, production, & post production.
Note: Must subscribe to get full stories.
http://www.hollywoodreporter.com

Moviemaker.com
Articles featuring interviews with top actors, directors, writers, producers, editors, and cinematographers. Links to resources and film festivals around the world.
http://www.moviemaker.com

Bibliography

A Subjective List of Useful Texts

A Subjective List of Useful Texts

Storyboards and Art Direction

Production Design and Art Direction Screencraft Peter Ettedgui; Focal Press, Woburn, MA, 1999

Pretty Pictures: Production Design and the History of Film C.S. Tashiro; University of Texas Press, Austin, TX, 1998

Sets in Motion: Art Direction and Film Narrative Charles Affron and Mirella Affron; Rutgers University Press, New Brunswick, NJ, 1995

What An Art Director Does: An Introduction to Motion Picture Production Design Ward Preston; Focal Press, Los Angeles, CA, 1994

By Design: Interviews With Film Designers Vincent Lobrutto; Praeger, Westport, CT, 1992

Masters of Light Schaefer and Salvato; University of California Press, Berkeley, CA, 1984

Film Architecture From Metropolis to Bladerunner Dietriech Neumann; Prestel, Munich, Germany, 1999

Drawing into Film: Director's Drawings The Pace Gallery, New York, NY, 1993 (op)

The Art of Hollywood: Fifty Years of Art Direction John Hambley and Patrick Downing.; Thames Television, London, England, 1979 (op)

Caligari's Cabinet and Other Illusions; A History of Film Design Leon Barsacq; New American Library, New York, NY, 1978

Theory/ Film Practice

Film Directing Shot by Shot: Visualizing from Concept to Screen Steven D. Katz; Michael Wiese Productions, Los Angeles, CA, 1991

FilmArt David Bordwell and Kristen Thompson; Addison Wesley, MA, 1979

Grammar of the Film Language Daniel Arijon; Silman-James Press, Los Angeles, CA, 1976

The Five C's of Cinematography Joseph V. Mascelli; Silman-James, Los Angeles, CA, 1998

Understanding Comics Scott McCloud; Harper Perenial, New York, NY, 1995

Film Form; Essays in Film Theory Sergei Eisenstein; Harcourt Brace – Jovanovich, New York, NY, 1987

Grammer of the Shot Roy Thompson; Focal Press, Oxford, England, 1998

Theory of the Film Bela Belazs; Dover, New York, NY, 1970

Film Directing

The Art of Alfred Hitchcock Donald Spoto; Doubleday and Co., New York, NY, 1976

Hitchcock/Truffaut Francois Truffaut; Simon and Schuster, New York, NY, 1983

The Act of Seeing Wim Wenders; Farber and Farber, London, England, 1992

Gilliam on Gilliam Terry Gilliam; Farber and Farber, London, England, 1999

Thinking in Pictures John Sayles; Houghton Mifflin, Boston, MA, 1987

Directing the Film: Film Directors on Their Art Eric Sherman; Acrobat Books Publishing, Los Angeles, CA, 1988

Something Like an Autobiography Akira Kurosawa; Vintage Books, New York, NY, 1983

A Cut Above: 50 Film Directors Talk About their Craft Michael Singer; Lone Eagle, Los Angeles, CA, 1998

Making Movies Work Jon Boorstin; Silman-James Press, Los Angeles, CA, 1995

Who the Devil Made It Peter Bogdonavich; Alfred Knopf, New York, NY, 1997

Hollywood Voices ed: Andrew Sarris, Bobs Merrill; New York, NY, 1971

On Directing Film David Mamet; Penguin USA, New York, NY, 1992

The World of Peter Greenaway Leon Steinmetz, Peter Greenway; Journey Editions, Boston, MA, 1995

Drawing

How to Draw Comics the Marvel Way Stan Lee and John Buscema; Simon and Schuster, Fireside Books, New York, NY, 1978

Drawing on the Right Side of the Brain Betty Edwards; J.P. Tarcher, Los Angeles, CA, 1979

The Natural Way to Draw Kimon Nicolades; Houghton Mifflin Company, Boston, MA, 1969

Perspective for Comic Book Artists David Chelsea; Watson-Guptill, New York, NY, 1997

Perspective Drawing, A Point of View Jane James; Prentice Hall, Englewood Cliffs, NJ, 1988

Perspective Drawing, An On-the-Spot Guide Mark Way; Outline Press, London, England, 1989

Reference

The Macmillan Visual Dictionary Jean-Claude Corbeil, ed.; Macmillan, New York, NY, 1992

The Complete Film Dictionary Ira Konigsberg; Meridian, Salinas, CA, 1987

The Story of Cinema David Shipman; St. Martin's Press, New York, NY, 1982

Credits

About the Author

Marcie Begleiter is a writer and educator who specializes in pre-visualization. She has worked extensively in the film, television, and interactive industries and is owner of Filmboards, whose client list includes Paramount, TriStar, New Line, and ABC. She is currently on the faculties of Art Center College of Design, the American Film Institute, and the new International Film School in Cologne, Germany. She has also been a featured lecturer at the Game Developer's Conference and Digital Video Expo, giving presentations on storyboarding and storytelling with images. She is a recipient of an NEA project grant, a FAR grant, and an Enrichment Grant from Art Center College.

Ms. Begleiter offers seminars on Storyboarding, Concept Development and Visual Narrative. For information on how to book seminars on these topics, please email Filmboards and Ms. Begleiter through the Filmboards Web site at:

mb@filmboards.com
www.filmboards.com

DIGITAL MOVIEMAKING
A Butt-Kicking, Pixel-Twisting Vision of the Digital Future and How to Make Your Next Movie on Your Credit Card

Scott Billups

You've got the script. You've got the vision. Now all you need is a deal to get your film made. But what if the powers-that-be say no? Do you have to give up your dream? Not any more. The digital revolution has made it cheaper and more possible than ever before for people to shoot and edit their own professional-quality films. This book will show you how to grab the bull by the horns and make your dream a reality.

Written for both experienced film and video directors who are new to the digital format and up-and-comers new to filmmaking in general, video guru Scott Billups' guide takes you through the brave new world of digital moviemaking. All the nuts-and-bolts information you need is right here, but technophobes need not fret. Billups explains in clear, concise, plain English what all these new terms and tools mean, and why it's not as hard as you think. He'll show you how to choose the technology that best fits your needs (and budget!) and how to get the maximum effect out of your equipment. Learn about different formats, effects tools, and cameras, as well as issues and challenges unique to shooting digitally.

Scott Billups has produced, directed, and written feature films, television programs, and commercials.

$26.95
Order # 2RLS
ISBN: 0-941188-30-2

DIGITAL FILMMAKING 101
An Essential Guide to
Producing Low-Budget Movies

Dale Newton and John Gaspard

The Butch Cassidy and the Sundance Kid of do-it-yourself filmmaking are back! Filmmakers Dale Newton and John Gaspard, co-authors of the classic how-to independent filmmaking manual *Persistence of Vision*, have updated their handbook for the digital age. *Digital Filmmaking 101* is your all-bases-covered guide to producing and shooting your own digital video films. It covers both technical and creative advice, from keys to writing a good script, to casting and location-securing, to lighting and low-budget visual effects. Also includes detailed information about how to shoot with digital cameras and how to use this new technology to your full advantage.

As indie veterans who have produced and directed three successful independent films, Gaspard and Newton are masters at achieving high-quality results for amazingly low production cost. They'll show you how to turn financial constraints into your creative advantage—and how to get the maximum mileage out of your production budget. You'll be amazed at the ways you can save money—and even get some things for free—without sacrificing any of your final product's quality.

Dale Newton and John Gaspard, who hail from Minneapolis, Minnesota, have produced three ultra-low-budget, feature-length movies and have lived to tell the tale.

$24.95
Order # 17RLS
ISBN: 0-941188-33-7

THE WRITER'S JOURNEY
2nd Edition
Mythic Structure for Writers

Christopher Vogler

See why this book has become an international best-seller and a true classic. First published in 1992, *The Writer's Journey* explores the powerful relationship between mythology and storytelling in a clear, concise style that's made it required reading for movie executives, screenwriters, scholars, and fans of pop culture all over the world.

Both fiction and nonfiction writers will discover a set of useful myth-inspired storytelling paradigms (i.e., "The Hero's Journey") and step-by-step guidelines to plot and character development. Based on the work of Joseph Campbell, *The Writer's Journey* is a must for all writers interested in further developing their craft.

The updated and revised 2nd Edition provides new insights, observations, and film references from Vogler's ongoing work on mythology's influence on stories, movies, and man himself.

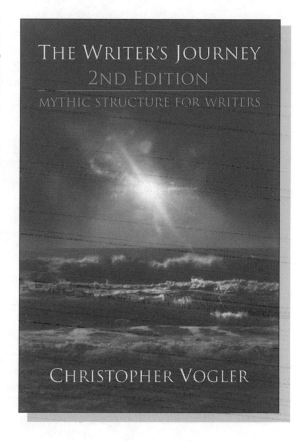

Christopher Vogler, a top Hollywood story consultant and development executive, has worked on such high-grossing feature films as The Lion King *and* The Thin Red Line *and conducts writing workshops around the globe.*

$22.95
Order # 98RLS
ISBN: 0-941188-70-1

FILM DIRECTING: SHOT BY SHOT
Visualizing from Concept to Screen

Steven D. Katz

This classic with the famous blue cover is one of the most well-known books in the business, and is a favorite of working directors as an on-set quick-reference guide. Packed with visual techniques for filmmakers and screenwriters to expand their stylistic knowledge, this international best-seller contains in-depth information on composition, previsualization, camera techniques, and much more. Includes over 750 storyboards and illustrations, with never-before-published storyboards from Spielberg's *Empire of the Sun*, Welles' *Citizen Kane*, and Hitchcock's *The Birds*.

$27.95
Order # 7RLS
ISBN: 0-941188-10-8

Both Katz Books Only $47
Save 12% when you order both books
Order #KatzB

....

FILM DIRECTING: CINEMATIC MOTION
A Workshop for Staging Scenes

Steven D. Katz

This follow-up to the phenomenally popular *Shot by Shot* is a practical guide to common production problems encountered when staging and blocking film scenes. Includes discussions of scheduling, staging without dialogue, sequence shots, actor and camera choreography, and much more. Also includes interviews with well-known professionals such as director John Sayles and visual effects coordinator Van Ling (*The Abyss*, *Terminator 2*).

$24.95
Order # 6RLS
ISBN: 0-941188-14-0

DIRECTING ACTORS
Creating Memorable Performances
for Film & Television

Judith Weston

The most important relationship on a movie set is between director and actor. The director is responsible for telling the story and the actors are responsible for bringing the story to life. *Directing Actors* is a method for establishing creative, mutually beneficial relationships between actors and directors. Using simple, practical tools that both directors and actors can use immediately, this book will show you how to get the most out of rehearsals, troubleshoot poor performances, and give directions that are clear, succinct, and easy to follow.

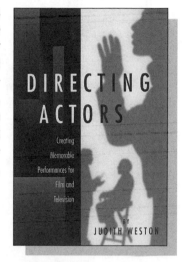

$26.95
Order # 4RLS
ISBN: 0-941188-24-8

SETTING UP YOUR SHOTS
Great Camera Moves Every Filmmaker Should Know

Jeremy Vineyard

Written in straightforward, non-technical language and laid out in a nonlinear format with self-contained chapters for easy reference, *Setting Up Your Shots* is like a Swiss army knife for filmmakers! Using examples from over 140 popular films, this book provides detailed descriptions of more than 100 camera setups, angles, and techniques. An excellent primer for beginning filmmakers and students of film theory, as well as a handy quick-reference guide for working filmmakers.

Contains 150 references to the great shots in your favorite films, including *2001: A Space Odyssey*, *Blue Velvet*, *The Matrix*, *The Usual Suspects*, *Vertigo* and more.

$19.95
Order # 8RLS
ISBN: 0-941188-73-6

DIRECTING 101

Ernest Pintoff

Written by one of the most respected and versatile filmmakers in the business, *Directing 101* takes a broad look at the process of directing. All the basics are here, from selecting and acquiring material to communicating with cast and crew, plus budgeting, production planning, filming techniques and more. A veteran of the movie business for nearly five decades, Pintoff shares the wisdom he's gleaned from years of working in film, animation, and television.

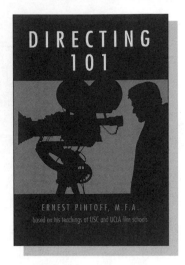

$16.95
Order # 40RLS
ISBN: 0-941188-67-1

THE DIRECTOR'S JOURNEY
The Creative Collaboration Between Director, Writer and Actor

Mark W. Travis

Although the director gets most of the credit for a film's creative vision, he or she is actually the center of a creative team that includes actors, writers, designers, producers, and editors, to name only a few. How do you draw all these artists together to realize a single vision? *The Director's Journey* helps directors master the art of collaboration, one of the most important skills a director can possess. Learn how to communicate your vision to the various crew members who will be carrying out your instructions while adding their own artistic touches to the mix. Includes discussions on melding the writer's vision with the director's vision, casting and working with actors, and using music, voiceover narration, and sound effects to enhance dramatic effect.

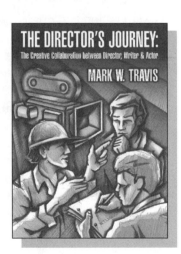

$26.95
Order # 29RLS
ISBN: 0-941188-59-0

INDEPENDENT FILM & VIDEOMAKER'S GUIDE
2nd Edition
Expanded & Updated

Michael Wiese

The new, completely expanded and revised edition of one of our best-sellers has all the information you need, from fundraising to distribution. This practical and comprehensive book will help filmmakers save time and money and inspire them to create successful projects.

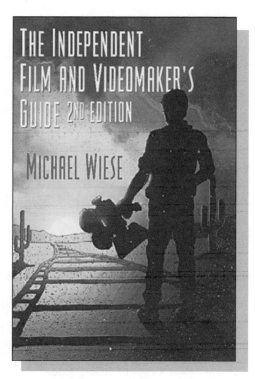

Contents include:

- Writing a business plan
- Developing your ideas into concepts, treatments, and scripts
- Directing, producing, and market research
- Understanding distribution markets (theatrical, home video, television, international)
- Financing your film
- Making presentations and writing a prospectus

Plus, an appendix filled with film cash flow projections, sample contracts, valuable contact addresses, and much more.

Using the principles outlined in this book, Wiese recently co-directed the short film *Field of Fish*, and is currently preparing his Bali feature. Additionally, Wiese is national spokesperson for Kodak's Emerging Filmmakers Program. He has conducted workshops on independent filmmaking in England, Germany, Finland, Indonesia, Ireland, Canada, Australia, and throughout the U.S. Contact Wiese at mw@mwp.com.

$29.95
Order # 37RLS
ISBN: 0-941188-57-4

ORDER FORM

MICHAEL WIESE PRODUCTIONS
11288 VENTURA BLVD., # 821
STUDIO CITY, CA 91604
E-MAIL: MWPSALES@MWP.COM
WEB SITE: WWW.MWP.COM

WRITE OR FAX FOR A FREE CATALOG

PLEASE SEND ME THE FOLLOWING BOOKS:

TITLE	ORDER NUMBER (#RLS _____)	AMOUNT
_____	_____	_____
_____	_____	_____
_____	_____	_____
_____	_____	_____
_____	_____	_____
	SHIPPING	_____
	CALIFORNIA TAX (8.00%)	_____
	TOTAL ENCLOSED	_____

PLEASE MAKE CHECK OR MONEY ORDER PAYABLE TO:

MICHAEL WIESE PRODUCTIONS

(CHECK ONE) ___ MASTERCARD ___VISA ____AMEX

CREDIT CARD NUMBER _____

EXPIRATION DATE _____

CARDHOLDER'S NAME _____

CARDHOLDER'S SIGNATURE _____

SHIP TO:

NAME _____

ADDRESS _____

CITY _____ STATE _____ ZIP _____

COUNTRY _____ TELEPHONE _____